Goals
For
Change

Goals
For
Change

How to Create
Your Ideal Life

Bob Colley
Toatfly Publishing

Individual orders for paperback and ebooks and bulk orders for PTAs, graduation classes, sales promotional use and corrections institutions can be found at:

www.GoalsForChange.com/ordering

Book design: Jim Bisakowski., BookDesign.ca

Edited by: Anne Correia, West Coast Editing Services

This book is dedicated to all of you who have the courage and determination to follow your dreams regardless of the obstacles, and to William, my son and the biggest influence in my life.

"If you keep a goal on the front burner, it's eventually going to come to a boil."

~Bob Colley

"If you aim at nothing, you'll hit it every time."

~Author Unknown

Also by the Author

Goals for Change web site:
www.GoalsForChange.com
Get free downloads to help you organize your goals along with ordering information.

Blog Your Goals
"Join, Share, Inspire"
www.BlogYourGoals.com
Learn to blog for frce and share your journey, your successes and even your failures to help others in their own quests.

Sleep Junkie
www.SleepJunkie.com
A blog that looks at sleep problems and possible cures.

Contents

Introduction

I've tried many programs that were designed to help a person outline their goals in order to make a plan for their life. Most of these resources are well written and they seemed like an excellent starting point. But I always found that they suffered from the same tragic flaw. They require that you start with a blank piece of paper, they'll ask some questions and you have to come up will a hundred goals on your own.

What I found difficult was that I often had to know what I didn't know in order to complete the basic outline. And I didn't know it!

One program instructed me to sit down in front of a piece of paper and I was given 20 minutes to let my mind run wild and write down anything that came up. I had to write as fast as I could without stopping.

After 20 minutes, my time was up and I was to have my list of 100 goals written out. I looked down at my piece of paper and found I had written 12. Needless to say I was very discouraged – I crumpled up that paper, tossed it in the trash and didn't try again for years.

When I first worked through the exercises described in this book it took me weeks to come up with 30 or so goals for what I wanted to have, what I wanted to do and the person I wanted to be. There were no ready resources to help me complete these basic lists and I came close to giving up many times.

Over time my personal lists grew into hundreds of items that I thought would help others complete their own list of goals. Why get hung up staring at a blank piece of paper when you can go through a list of items and just pick what appeals to you?

This book isn't packed with a bunch of places to see or things to eat. You're not going to write a mission statement or read countless questions and have to brainstorm a list of ideas by yourself.

This book is about getting through the process quickly so you can get on with the most important part, that of making it all come true by living the life you always wanted.

The one thing you never want for yourself is a bucket list that you never get to. It's important to have dreams, but why wait to do all the things you've always wanted to try?

If you think you don't have time to read this book, ask yourself, "Where will I be 1, 5 or 10 years from now?" If you see yourself in the same rut you're in now, then commit to replacing an hour or two a day of TV, gaming or time-sucking social networking sites with creating the life you were meant to live.

All you really need to get the most out of this book is to download the blank forms from www.GoalsForChange.com or a dollar store note book and a pen. Then spend whatever time you have available to go through each section.

It's easiest to follow the sections as they are presented in the book but feel free to jump to any part that interests you. The lists included in the chapters are not exhaustive, but they are intended to get you thinking about what you want for your own life. If something sounds great to you, then write it down exactly as it appears. Or, if the idea sounds good but not exactly right, add your own spin to it so that it's meaningful to you. Even an idea that doesn't work for you could get you thinking about what *does* work.

This isn't a test, so have fun, put your feet up and create a vision for your life that will excite and inspire you.

Chapter One

Things to Have

Introduction

This section is one you will enjoy, as it will help you become clear on the things that you want to have. It will also help you become excited about the possibilities that await you and assist you later in creating ways to bring all the things you desire into your life.

This is the time for you to let your imagination run wild. Don't worry about how you will afford any of your treasures, as you will come up with that later. So dream big and imagine you have unlimited money, unlimited time and unlimited ability to get whatever it is you want in your life. Use the following suggestions as items you can add to your list, or use them as a starting point for items you come up with yourself.

Go Soak in a Hot Tub

You'll want one that comes with as many jets as possible, and a stereo system you can plug your mp3 player into that plays the sound even underwater.

It'll also come with mood lighting and a small waterfall. It should also have a slide-up, wireless TV and a floating remote.

Wrap your hot tub in a cedar gazebo with big windows and skylights. Oh, and a mini bar in the corner.

This is just what is needed for peace, relaxation and to relieve the stress and tension at the end of the day.

Feel Marvellous in Your Designer Clothes

Armani, Diesel, Dior, Prada, Fendi and Malo start off the collection.

Shirts, shoes, dresses, belts, suits, ties, sunglasses and handbags are neatly displayed and easy to find in a humungous walk-in closet.

The problem now is deciding which fantastic clothes you'll wear to wow the masses.

Toss Your Glasses with Laser Eye Surgery

Get you eyeballs laser shaved so you can live without the glasses and forget about the contact lens mess and fuss. This can correct your vision and give you the 20/20 eyes that can get you into the space program.

It's been a few decades since the process was first created and the technology has advanced, so maybe it's time to save up and have the surgery.

This also isn't the time to go cheap. Find a company with a solid track record, and if the surgeon is wearing glasses, move on to another one.

An Out-of-This World Meteorite

You could be watching the heavens just as a meteor lights up the night sky and flames through the atmosphere and crashes to earth. You could be the first on the scene and have the chance to name it. Usually they're named after where it was found, not after your dog.

Maybe you can find one of these celestial bodies that have survived an impact with the earth and have been lying undiscovered for thousands of years among your local rocks.

Your Ideal House

Your place may be a waterfront estate with an ocean view or a dock on a lake, or in the woods, on a mountain by a meandering stream, a penthouse condo downtown or acreage with a vineyard and organic produce.

You can have a cosy retreat or a monster house. It can come with a garden and a large backyard or a penthouse view over the city.

Your house can come with a pool, tennis court, indoor gym, an art studio, a putting green, games room, a home theatre and a guest house.

Search the internet for your ideal house. It's either out there or there's something close that can be fixed up with a gob of cash.

Set of Fine Silverware

Toss the motley collection that's never had even two matching pieces. Enjoy a set of fine silverware with a timeless, graceful pattern. Don't save it for special occasions but use it every day and experience elegant dining at every meal.

An Exotic Sports Car

Sit behind the wheel of a Ferrari, Lamborghini, Aston Martin, Bugatti, Lotus or Porsche and rip down the open road.

A great thing to have but you'll need deep pockets for a car that can start at a few hundred thousand dollars and reach into the millions.

A Classic Collector Car

Maybe a Ford Model A, a 1930 Cadillac V16 or '26 Durant. How about a classic muscle car like the Torino Cobra, Pontiac LeMans, Corvette Stingray, Camaro or a Mustang Mach 1.

You could specialize in American or European cars, convertibles or have a little of everything.

If you would like a Jay Leno type of collection, you'll need an aircraft hangar-sized garage.

An Artistic Masterpiece

Some artwork from the 16th, 17th or 18th century or something from the Renaissance. How would a Picasso, Van Gogh or Monet look on you walls?

As some of these can go for 10's of millions a few from a lesser known artist would do. Try some reproductions to start out.

You could have a collection of sculptures in stone, ceramic or porcelain.

An RV for Travelling the Country

It can be a truck camper, a travel trailer, a tent trailer, a fifth wheel or a motor home.

Your head will spin with all the options and floor plans.

Join up with a club and travel together.

A Black Yukon XL Denali or Suburban
They are the vehicle of choice for cops, drug cartel leaders and rap celebrities. They're big, powerful and very comfortable. Maybe a Cadillac Escalade.

Get one with a flex fuel V8, autoride suspension, a heated steering wheel, a Bose surround sound luxury stereo system and power everything.

Classic Wooden Cruiser
Own a classic wood cruiser from Chris Craft, Egg Harbor, Trojan, Pacemaker, Matthews, Trumpy or Ditchburn.

Yacht
Sailing or power? Do you want something to fool around in on the lake or to travel the high seas? Should it sleep two, six or a few dozen of your closest friends?

Boathouse
A garage on the water will protect your boat from the suns rays and keep the rain out. You'll also have a spot to store all your boat-related gear.

You can have your boathouse at a marina or it can be at the end of your own dock.

Go Kart
Race your own go kart around your local track. It might be the start of your racing career.

Indoor Pool

Get up in the morning and go for a swim in your indoor pool. You don't have to worry about what the weather is like, there are no leaves to clean out and it's available anytime you want.

Outdoor pool

Sit on a lounge chair beside your outdoor pool reading a book, having a cool drink; then jump into your pool when things get too hot.

Chic Hut

Your own private cedar room in the back yard where you can go to get away from it all for a while. Light some candles, play some soft music and stretch out on your yoga mat.

Infrared Sauna

Have the heat of the sun without the sun to get you to a healthy sweat. A sauna can reduce stress, aches and pain and a few pounds of belly fat.

Get a model made of western red cedar or hemlock and make sure it comes with a CD/mp3 player so you can listen to some mood music or meditation music while you detoxify your body and improve your immune system.

You can fit a two-person model almost anywhere, or get a four- to six-person model with enough room for you to lie down on the bench.

Dishwasher

It doesn't matter whether it's a portable or built-in model as they are both great. It really is convenient to load it up, turn it on and take out the clean dishes an hour later.

With a dishwasher the counter around the sink area stays clean and uncluttered. That leaves plenty of space for making snacks or monster sandwiches.

$10 Million in the Bank
Nothing takes the pressure off like 10 million dollars in the bank. You can easily live off the interest and use it to do anything and to go anywhere you want.

Sports Car
For everyday driving or to impress, how about a Dodge Viper SRT10, a Ford Shelby GT500, a Chevy Corvette or a Pontiac Solstice.

Gold Rim China Place Settings
Decide between bone china and porcelain then check out some makes like Royal Doulton, Wedgwood, Mikasa, Waterford or Faberge.

Then set an elegant table everyone will compliment you on.

A Fully Equipped Exercise Room
Get a great cardio workout, lose weight and build some muscle in your own exercise room. No more excuses or standing in line at the gym to use a sweaty piece of equipment.

A Big Workshop with All the Very Best Tools
A separate building at least 2000 square feet in size should do it. There'll be room for every power tool you could ever want – even if you don't ever use them or know what they even does.

Add a dust collection system, a winch, 220 power and a wood stove in the corner and you can hunker down in your man (or woman!) cave all weekend long.

A Cedar Strip Kayak or Canoe
You could get a plastic sit-on, but why not go for a classic looking cedar strip kayak. Build it yourself from a kit or have it professionally made for you.

Kayaking Gear
You want to be in the water with gear that will keep you comfortable, as dry as possible and safe.

You can cruise the quiet morning water around an island, out with the whales, down a river or crashing through the waves.

Well-Crafted Wood Furniture
A house with custom wood furniture is a joy to admire and use. If cared for it can also last generations.

Make sure it's all solid wood from a reputable maker. You can't go wrong with oak, cherry, maple, black walnut, beech or white ash.

A Touring Motorcycle
Sit upright on a Harley-Davidson, Yamaha or Triumph. Or you can make your own.

A Crotch Rocket Motorcycle
A sport bike from Kawasaki, Honda or Ducati will get you there before you even know where you want to go.

Your Own Plane

How cool would flying your own plane be? It could be a turbo prop or a jet engine model.

Land at an air strip, on the water or on a snow-covered tundra.

Take your family and friends on a weekend trip.

Top of the Line Gaming PC

Set yourself up with a gigabit LAN, a multi-TB hard drive, 10 GB RAM, a GIG video card and a bleeding edge processor. Match it up with a monster 1080p LCD monitor, camera, joystick, steering wheel and foot pedals.

Or course you'll have to upgrade every three to six months.

BMX Bike

Ride for fun on your own BMX bike. Maybe you could change things up with a mountain bike?

Best Gaming Consoles

You can't have just one so you'll need an Xbox 360, a Playstation, and a Nintendo Wii that are all wireless with controllers for all. You'll need an empty wall so you'll have somewhere to shelve every game that's ever been made worth having.

MP3 Player

An mp3 player matched with a top of the line sound isolating/noise-cancelling earphones so you can hear your music like you were there.

eReader

Keep up with your favourite authors on your Palm OS, Nintendo e-Reader, a Kindle or Sony reader.

iPhone

Get the latest iPhone and load it up with every app they have – play games, keep track of the stock market, read a book, keep connected to your social networking sites, track your expenses and tons more.

Oh, and it also makes phone calls.

Snowboard Gear

Get a snowboard, boots, bindings, jacket, pants, gloves, goggles and a helmet to protect your brain.

A season's pass at a first rate resort will make winters enjoyable and fun.

Your Own Chalet

You can drive up on a Friday evening and spend the weekend skiing or snowboarding right out your front door.

You can bring a group of friends along and you can rent it out when you're not using it.

In the right area, it can also be fantastic as a summer getaway for some mountain biking.

Home Theatre System

There's no need to watch a movie on a tiny 52 inch screen when your home theatre can have a wall-sized screen. Combined with a booming sound system, some leather recliners, a popcorn maker and a fridge for refreshments it will sure beat going to any movie theatre.

Four-Poster Bed
Spend your nights sleeping in an opulent four-poster bed.

Set of Ping Golf Clubs
A golf bag filled with Ping gold clubs will set you apart on the golf course. You're using what the pros use and even if you're just a weekend warrior, you'll be able to slice into the next fairway in style.

Hiking Gear
You'll have a comfortable pair of waterproof leather boots, clothing to keep you warm and dry and a tent for overnight and multi-day trips in the back country.

Your hikes can be an afternoon or a week long.

Camping Gear
You'll need a stove, cookware, lights, maybe a navigation unit and a backpack to haul all your gear.

Or you can do car camping. Fill your vehicle with a tent, sleeping bags, clothes, a cooler and some food and you can drive right into your camp site.

Unload and set up your tent in no time. Then relax in a lawn chair or head down to the lake for a swim.

Guest Cottage
Having room in your own house to kick back and relax and entertain friends is great, but when relatives come to stay is would be even better to put them up in their own place. That will be your guest cottage that is set off from your house on your property.

Your guests can have their privacy and you can have yours. You also don't have to worry about them going through your drawers and pawing your stuff.

Collection of Antiques

You could collect works of art, furniture, pottery, watches or coins.

Wood Chipper

A wood chipper is a great way to reduce a mountain of garden waste down to a small pile that can be put in your composters or spread around your yard to help your plants grow.

It's fun to feed branches into the chipper and have them come out the other end in little pieces. And the machine also makes lots of noise, which can be an end in itself.

Motocross Bike

Ride trails or a track at breakneck speeds.

Guitar

Get a guitar and learn how to play it. It can be an acoustic or an electric model.

Taking lessons or learning from a friend that already plays well will make the leaning process that much easier. If you just try to learn from a book, you'll get frustrated and quit. And you will have to put in years of practice.

You can play just for the enjoyment or you can make a living playing in front of an audience.

Piano

You can have an electric model in your apartment, an upright or grand model in your house.

Compose your own music, play for friends and family or just lose yourself in a song during some private time.

Drums

A great way to get in touch with your inner tribal self is with a set of drums. You may want bongos, a hand drum that is used in a culture you are interested in or a complete drum set to start your own rock band.

Mountain bike

Get a mountain bike or an all terrain bike for some off-road cycling. Go through the forest, along dirt trails, over jumps and through creeks. Or maybe your thing is going down a mountain at break-neck speed.

A bike with front and rear suspension will help keep your kidneys in place.

There are a lot of different kinds of bikes to choose from so match the bike to the kinds of terrain you'll be riding.

A Business

Why start a business when you could buy one or several?

Riding Lawn Mower

A riding mower sure beats pushing a mower around a large yard. Sit back and cruise around with a cool beverage and get your yard looking great in no time.

Skateboard and a Halfpipe

Have a collection of skateboards to ride on your own half-pipe in your backyard.

Deck Box

Either on the back deck or on the patio by the pool, a deck box is great for storing outdoor stuff in one place. Store your cushions out of the rain, towels and table cloths and a few of the kid's toys.

A deck box can be plastic or made out of a wood like cedar to match your deck.

Cedar Deck

Walk out your back door onto your cedar deck and sit down and relax after a tough morning interviewing bauble polishers.

Your deck spills onto your lawn, overlooks a forest, the ocean or meadow. Add a sun shade and it's a great place be when outside.

Gas BBQ

You may want one that can cook a whole steer or a good, family-sized model could suit you just fine. Your BBQ should come with heavy grates for searing your steaks, a rotisserie and a light source for evening cooking.

You can run it off tanks or a gas line from your house. Choose between one that burns charcoal or wood.

Indulge your primal urges.

Housekeeper/Maid

Since you don't want to be spending your time with routine house maintenance like cleaning bathrooms, dusting and vacuuming, you'll have to hire someone to do it for you.

Depending on the size of your place, you could have live-in help or someone who comes over once or twice a week.

Wood Sauna

A cedar sauna by the outdoor pool is a wonderful place to sweat away the stress of the day.

You can get one with an electric heater or, if you have more time, a wood heater.

GPS for the Car/Truck

A global positioning system can get you from your front door to that rented cabin in the woods or across town to a lunch date at a new restaurant. There is now no need for a paper map, which is great because no one can refold them anyway.

Chain Saw

A chain saw is great for trimming up some trees around your house or cottage and for cutting up a pile of fire wood.

Most of the time you really don't need one but they're loud, can destroy stuff and are dangerous, so what's not to love?

Wood Stove

You can now get wood stoves that are a lot more energy efficient and cleaner than they used to be. They are great to sit around on a winter's day, to snuggle in front of with a lover, or just to indulge your pyromaniac tendencies.

A wood stove with a flat top can also provide a place to heat up water or food if the power ever goes out. One with a glass front can provide enough light to play a board game or read a book.

A Multimedia Server

Store all your movies, MP3 music and pictures on a wireless, monstrous server so you can access anything you want from anywhere in your house.

Stream a movie to your TV by the pool or music to your games room.

Pool Table

An eight foot pool table and a rack of cues can make for a fun evening with friends.

Dune Buggy

Fly over the dunes at your local beach with your own dune buggy. Or take it for some off-road action in the back woods.

Foosball Table

Foosball is indoor soccer played with players on rods that you spin around to kick a ball into your opponent's net.

Play for fun at your place or practice up for tournament play. Side bets are encouraged.

Pinball Machine

A couple of classic flipper-activated games are still fun especially if you don't have to keep pumping in quarters.

Games Room

Have a separate room in your house for all your gaming systems, pool table, foosball table and old style pinball machines. Even out your games collection with a few electronic games.

A fridge to keep some refreshments cold and some soundproofing will complete the effect.

Home Office
A separate room to take care of business is what you'll need. Complete with a large desk, telephone, fax and computer, you can pay the bills, write a best seller and keep tabs on your stock portfolio.

Jet Ski
Spend your summer hours on the water on your own jet ski. Get one that goes faster than your ability to think ahead.

Wine Cellar
With your own wine cellar you can age the wine you buy to make it even better. Pick up two cases of each wine you like. The first one is for your immediate consumption and the second one goes into your wine cellar for a few years.

You can keep a few bottles of wine for special occasions and for collecting.

Instant Hot Water System
You can save big money on your energy costs with a tankless water heating system that provides instant hot water just when you need it.

No more running the tap for a few minutes to get hot water or constantly washing your hands in ice water.

Club Memberships
Get a membership at a golf club, yacht club, tennis club or a health club. How about one at a martial arts school or community arts group?

A Dock
Build a nice, large and stable dock on the water for parking your boat, swimming or for sitting by the water's edge to enjoy a summer day.

It can be on a river, a lake or an ocean and at your house or cottage.

A Large Garden
You can grow your own vegetables, flowers, annuals or perennials. Set aside a spot for some fresh herbs, roses and exotic plants.

Grow your plants in large beds or in containers. It is a relaxing hobby with an endless variety of plants and garden designs.

Greenhouse
Start off your outdoor plants or grow your plants all year round in your own greenhouse. Or maybe yours is for tropical plants, orchids or a home for your butterfly collection.

Snowmobile
Ride the trails in winter on your own snowmobile. Join a group and tour the back woods.

Five Car Garage
You'll need a five car garage to keep your sports car, truck, SUV, everyday grocery-getter and luxury car.

Your Own Island

Get away from the crowds and truly experience peace and privacy with your own island.

Tennis Court

Have a tennis court right out in your yard so you can have a game whenever the urge hits you.

Set up a backboard or get a ball launcher for your practice sessions.

Paintball Gear

Get the fastest paintball maker there is and you and your friends can have a blast in the woods playing capture the flag.

Surround Sound Stereo System

Get a receiver and an amplifier matched up with a set up speakers that will blow your mind with incredible sound. A good way to get to know your neighbours.

Sailboat

You can get a sailboat for short day trips around the bay or a larger sailboat for open ocean voyages. The world can be yours.

Motorboat

You need something for fishing so a motorboat designed for this purpose will get plenty of use.

Get yourself a boat around 18-20 feet with twin outboard motors that can get you to where the fish are before they know you're coming.

Canoe
You can paddle a quiet lake for a few hours or race down a river with a canoe loaded with gear for a multi-day adventure.

All Terrain Vehicle
Own an ATV that you can take on some backcountry trails, through a few creek beds and over a mound of rocks. The muddiest person wins.

Sailboard
You basically have a sail on a surf board. It is like a sailboat you can take almost anywhere there are water and some wind.

Personal Water Craft
Jump some waves in your PWC, visit wildlife or even do a little fishing.

Season's Tickets
Get season's ticket to your favourite sport team.

Snowmobile
You can take almost all the same trails in the winter with your snowmobile as you did in the summer with your ATV. Join up with a group.

4x4 for Off-Roading
This beast will have huge tires and enough ground clearance to go over boulders bigger than a buffalo. These machines are meant to get dirty, scratched and dinged on their way along a trail at low speed so you can show off your driving skill.

Or get a super-charged version for racing through the desert.

Luxury Car
Drive a Cadillac, Lincoln, or anything that is big and filled with leather.

Compact Car
This is the car you take on errands around town and to the supermarket. It's fuel efficient and environmentally friendly.

Jewellery
Fill your life with diamonds, gold and jewels. They can be bracelets, rings, pendants, earrings, cufflinks, or necklaces.

Luxury Watch
These go way beyond telling time. Some can cost more than many people make in a year or even a lifetime. Go ahead and get two.

Dirt Bike
Have yourself a little fun roaring through the trails on a dirt bike.

Luxury Pen
You'll need a fine writing instrument for signing your autograph.

Slow Cooker
Spend a few minutes preparing your food in the morning and put it in a slow cooker. When you come home at the end of the day you have a nutritious, home-cooked meal ready for you.

Set of Knives
It will be a joy to own a finely balanced set of stainless steel knives for working in the kitchen.

Patio Furniture
A comfortable set of chairs and tables for the patio. And throw in an umbrella to provide some shade.

An Organic Garden
You can grow your own food in your own organic garden. Vegetables, fruits and herbs are easy to grow in a garden or even in pots.

Wireless Network in Your Home
Have a wireless network in your home so all your computers can communicate with each other, share files and printers and stream music and videos to wherever you want them.

Digital Camera
You can own a digital camera with a zoom lens and extra memory to store your photos. You'll also need a supply of nine million batteries.

Microwave Oven
Get a microwave oven that can also bake and broil and you can heat up a delicious meal in no time.

Luggage
Get a set of sturdy, matching luggage to bring on your many trips.

Pet

Get a cat, dog, fish, horse, or mongoose as a pet for company and as a source of unconditional love. Just make sure there's food in the bowl.

Utility Trailer

You can haul top soil, gravel, sod, yard waste or construction materials in your own utility trailer.

Moped

There is no license required to drive one of these little scooters and they can be rechargeable or run on a small amount of gas.

Conclusion

I hope you have created an exciting list of the things you would like to have. Some of the things you may get fairly quickly and others may take some time. Not to worry as that's all part of the grand design.

Next up you will create a list of the things you want to do in your life.

———·•·———

Chapter Two

Things to Do

Introduction

Now that your notebook has a page or more of the things you want, it's time to focus on the things you want to do.

You could go on exotic trips, write a children's book, learn to play the piano or help build a school in a third world country. Act like everything is possible and don't hold back because of any fears or self limitations.

Use the following suggestions for your list or as a start to create ideas of your own.

The following are some of the things that can make getting out of bed in the morning a joy.

Discover an Inexpensive, Renewable Energy Source

Figure out how to harness $E=MC^2$ and you can run a car on a handful of gravel or maybe those little marshmallows. How about inventing an engine that runs on gravity or one powered by neutrinos? Can you figure out how to harness the energy from lightning?

Our society needs a quantum leap in this area. Maybe it could be you.

Run a Half Marathon
If you're jogging already, slowly increase your distance. If you're just beginning, joining a group might be the way to go.

You can start out running a 5K race, then a 10K and then a half marathon. Train and then go for it. Maybe you can run a full marathon next time or even a biathlon or triathlon. Extreme marathoners are insane.

Go for a Zero-G Ride
A trip on a space shuttle or a Soviet rocket would be the ultimate, but a flight on a plane making parabolic arcs that leave you floating in "space" would still be cool. For a few hours at 30 seconds at a time you can experience what space flight would be like.

Hit a Hole in One
You may have to start playing golf 3-5 times per week and if you keep at it, one of these days you'll get a hole in one.

You'll watch the ball roll up the green and fall into the cup. The rest of your foursome won't believe it, but you knew it was going to happen.

Meditate Every Morning
Set aside a special place and twenty minutes to sit quietly, concentrating on your breath and quieting your mind. If thoughts intrude on your solitude, just dismiss them and bring your concentration back to your breath.

There are many way to practice meditation so try a few until you find the one that works best for you.

Have Your Dream Wedding

Have some friends help you plan your dream wedding. Get design ideas for gowns, your jewellery, the cake, catering, flowers, limo and your vows. Never ask the groom-to-be his opinion on anything as it will be pointless.

Swim with a Great White Shark

You can travel down south and scuba dive or snorkel with sharks. You can swim with some sharks unprotected, and for others you'd better be in a shark cage. It will sure be a better story than telling your friends back home that you just sat on the beach for your vacation.

Trip to a Pole

You can have an adventure going to either the North Pole or the South Pole. You can go there by air or by sea. If you're really fit, you can try to ski there. You can leave your swim trunks at home.

Meet and Marry Your Ideal Mate

Get an idea in your mind of your ideal mate. What would they look like? How would they act? What qualities would they have? Then get out of the house and be open to what life has to offer.

Go Parachuting

You can do a free fall skydive or take a tandem jump strapped to an instructor. Check out several companies and bring a friend along – you don't want to do something this insane alone.

Go Whale Watching

You can go out in a cruiser or speed around in a zodiac to where the whales are. Head out for a few hours and get an unforgettable view of a killer whale. You'll probably also see some seals, porpoises and bald eagles too.

Hike Mount Kilimanjaro

Located in Tanzania, Mount Kilimanjaro is the highest peak in Africa. Plan on taking a week to a week and a half to complete your trek up to the snow-capped Uhuru peak at 19,341 feet. This time also includes a few days before and after and the climb itself.

New Year's Eve in Times Square

Stand in Times Square as the New Year's Eve Ball descends and cheer the New Year in with a million other revellers. Get to Broadway early for a spot to see the ball.

Read the Entire Bible and Koran

You don't have to become a religious scholar, but try reading a few pages every night. It may take you a few years but true understanding takes time.

Write a Best Selling Book

You could write a children's book, a detective novel, a how-to book or a book about anything you like. If you want it to be a best seller, make it about something a lot of other people would be interested in.

If you can write only a few pages a day, in a year your book will be done. You can sell your manuscript to a publisher or self publish your masterpiece.

Be in the Olympics

The Olympics are held every four years in the summer and in the winter. If you are an athlete on the top of your game you can go as a competitor.

You can buy tickets to see some of the events or you could get in free by volunteering to help out.

Set a World Record

Run faster, jump farther or eat more than anyone else and you can set a world record. Your achievement can be sports related or absolutely whacky.

Flip through the book of Guinness World Records and find something you and a crowd can do, or make up your own event. How about the loudest R&R song ever played?

Maintain an Exercise Program

Find something you like and keep with it. You can lift weights, run, play a sport or even go for a walk every day.

Remember to start off slowly and gradually build up so you don't hurt yourself.

Attain and Maintain Your Ideal Weight

This may be one of the hardest things you can do but it will pay the most dividends. If your ideal height for your weight is 15 feet, you will have to lose a few pounds.

If you have to lose a lot of weight, take it easy and reduce gradually. You didn't gain the weight in a month so it will take a lot longer to lose it.

This will take a lifestyle adjustment. Just going on a fad diet will not keep you from regaining any weight you lost on the diet when you go back to your old eating habits.

Learn How to Draw

Take a course and learn how to draw people, cartoons, animals or objects. A course can be taken at a school or over the internet.

Learn How to Paint

You can paint using watercolours, acrylics or oils. It can be a relaxing hobby or you can sell your work to make a living.

Help Out at a Soup Kitchen

Volunteer to help out working at a soup kitchen serving meals to those in need, helping to prepare the meals, setting up tables or cleaning up afterwards.

Go to the Kentucky Derby

Put on a suit or wear a bizarre hat and be part of one the most classic horse races ever.

Be a Regular Blood Donor

Donating your blood can help someone who needs a transfusion because of an accident or an operation.

If you're healthy and able, make it a goal to give 50 pints.

Have a Grand Slam at Bridge

Bid and win all 13 tricks in a game of bridge.

Send a Message in a Bottle

You can try sending out a message in a bottle. Where will it end up? Who may find it? How long and how far will it travel?

Be an Extra in a Movie

There might be a movie shooting in your area and they could have a casting call for extras. You could be part of a crowd or, if you're really lucky, a dead body.

Sail on a Tall Ship

Out on the open sea, the enormous masts seem to reach the sky as the sails fill out with wind. You don't need to have any sailing skills – just a desire to learn and enjoyment of the adventure.

You can go on an afternoon trip, or on one that lasts for more than a year.

Learn to Sing

Join a local group or choir and learn how to sing. Maybe you could be on a reality show and become the next recording star.

See the Rolling Stones in Concert

Or any other classic rock and roll band. The Stones are a good bet as they'll be touring well into their nineties.

Go on a River Cruise

Rent a boat and take a leisurely cruise down a European river.

Learn to Surf

Paddle out on your board, catch a wave and get stoked as you ride a fat wave all the way in without having to bail or get blasted, dude.

Be Athlete of the Week
Get your picture in the local paper for being the athlete of the week in your favourite sport.

Go to the Symphony
Listen to a classical toe tapper by Mozart, Beethoven or anyone with "ini" at the end of their name.

Go to the Opera
Watch singers, actors and dancers perform a dramatic work to music. Don't leave until the fat lady sings.

Be Interviewed by Oprah
You may be interviewed by Oprah on her new network show. You may have to start off with your local network station and work your way up.

Try Skiing or Snowboarding
Take some lessons and try it out. You may find a sport you'll love for your entire life.

Save an Injured Animal
Take an injured bird, dog or horse for medical care. Help push a whale or dolphin back out to sea.

Start a Business
You could buy a franchise or base your business on an idea or invention you created. It could be a one-person shop or evolve into a plant that employs thousands of people.

See a Wild Bear
Go on a tour that will take you into the bear's natural environment. See a grizzly, black, brown and polar bear. How about a panda to round things out?

Visit Space

You can be an astronaut or you could pay your way into space as a tourist. Prices are dropping from their 20 million dollar price tag to only a few hundred thousand. Book early, but be warned, if they lose your luggage you'll probably never see it again.

Visit Every Park in Your Hometown

Go for a stroll, a swing or a hike in all of the parks in or near your hometown. If your town has a tourist booth, pick up a brochure or two about your area and be a local tourist.

So many people have a wonderful collection of beautiful parks within a short distance of where they live but never visit them.

Go for a Hot Air Balloon Ride

Get to your balloon before sunrise and lift off for a silent drift over your town and the surrounding countryside.

Touch down in a field and enjoy a champagne toast to your adventure.

Meet Your Favourite Celebrity

Maybe you'll win a back stage pass or your idol is shooting a movie in your town.

Be respectful and polite. The stalking behaviour of the paparazzi won't be well received.

Ride in a Submarine

You can get a ride on small, personal-sized submarine, but if you look around and if you are important enough, you might get a ride on a large navy vessel.

Indoor Rock Climbing

Try some indoor rock climbing and see if you can make it all the way to the top of the wall. There's a safety line so if you fall off you'll be O.K.

See a Las Vegas Show

Go for a dinner package and you can enjoy a wonderful meal then see a musical, your favourite headliner, a comedian or a magician. They might even have a burlesque show or two in the city that never sleeps.

Visit the Pyramids

They're not making any more of them so go and see one of the last remaining seven wonders of the ancient world in Egypt.

Learn to Ride a Horse

You have to give it a try at least once. Go out on a trail ride. How about riding a camel or a donkey?

Swim with Dolphins

During a vacation to Florida or the Bahamas take an afternoon or a week and go swimming with dolphins either in a pool or out in the ocean.

Paddle a River

Paddle a canoe or kayak down a lazy river or one with class 3 rapids. Be a modern-day pioneer and explore the river's entire length.

Fly a Glider

Soar through the sky with the eagles, with the wind as the only sound around. Without an engine these planes use the thermals for lift.

Learn to Play a Musical Instrument

Learn to play the guitar, banjo, piano, flute, trumpet, didg-eridoo, violin, drums or any musical instrument you have an interest in.

The kazoo, spoons or washboard don't really cut it.

Enter a Bathtub Race

Hook up an outboard motor to a modified bathtub and see if you can go around the course the fastest to ring the bell at the end.

Try Paragliding

Jump off a cliff with a modified parachute and catch an air current. This is one of those things where training with an experienced paragliding expert would be a good idea.

Go to Church Every Week

Go to a church close to where you live and allow the reli-gious teachings to transform your mind and spirit.

Drink More Water

Everyone knows they should drink more water but few people ever do drink enough during the day to remain properly hydrated, keep the interior plumbing working ef-ficiently and help remove toxins from the body.

Set your watch to chime every hour and try to drink a cup of water before the next chime goes off. Aim for about 8 cups a day.

Keep a glass on your desk and a water bottle in your car or in hand when you go for a walk. Keeping hydrated can increase your energy level and reduce your intake of junk food and sugary drinks.

Quit Smoking

Breathing in over three thousand chemicals with every puff makes smoking a self-mutilation habit that you should quit as soon as you can.

Get some help from your doctor or see your pharmacist. It's never too late to stop.

Go on an African Safari

See lions, giraffes, zebras, elephants and more in their natural habitat. You can walk, drive or even do it with luxury camping.

Dance at a Powwow

Learn about the traditional Native American ceremony and join in the dance if you're invited.

Catch a Big Fish

Go on a fishing charter for tuna or marlin. Catch a fish that will make your typical hometown catch look like bait.

Try to Eat 50 Hard Boiled Eggs

See if you can equal the task achieved by Cool Hand Luke and eat 50 hard boiled eggs.

Practice Random Acts of Kindness

Hold the door for someone, let a person go ahead of you in the checkout line, pay the toll of the car behind you, pick up some trash off the street and throw it in a garbage can, put some money in a parking meter that's about to expire or buy a homeless person a meal.

Adopt a Pet from the SPCA

Help out your local animal shelter by buying an animal from them. When you want a pet in your life, visit a shelter for that special dog, cat or bunny and find a friend for life.

Bowl a Perfect Game

Bowl a game of all strikes. Choose 5 or 10 pin bowling. Or how about bowling a perfect game doing each?

Experience the Summer Solstice at Stonehenge

Partake in summer solstice among the over 5000-year-old stones in Britain that were erected for solar and lunar worship. The stones were placed by Druids, probably every time a Druid lost a bet playing Roll-The-Bones.

If you're really into it, you can build your own in a field on your property.

Dog Sled in the Arctic

Take the reins and run a dog sled over the ice and snow in Canada's Baffin Island or the Northwest Territories.

Learn to Read or Read Better

It's never too late to learn how to read. A local school can help. Reading can help you keep up with what is happening in the world and can open new doors of opportunity.

Maybe you can teach someone else how to read.

Earn a Degree

Go back to school and earn a high school or college degree.

Watch a Tennis Match at Wimbledon

Watch a professional tennis tournament played on the grass courts of Wimbledon in London, England, home to the oldest and most prestigious tennis tournament in the world.

Go River Rafting

There are places that have a gentle, family-fun ride and others where you'll hang on for dear life as you go down the river in a rubber raft.

Go to the Super Bowl

Experience the championship football game in person. It's a football fanatic requirement.

Go Indoor Skydiving

Try skydiving without having to jump out of a plane by doing it in a vertical wind tunnel.

Learn to Fly a Helicopter

In twelve to twenty-five weeks you can become a helicopter pilot. Flying can be challenging and fun, and you can land almost anywhere.

Sleep Under the Stars

When camping in the summer, set up your sleeping bag outside your tent and sleep under the stars. You can do this at a cottage or even in your own back yard. Far from any town or city is best as you will be able to see many more stars.

Watch a Building Being Imploded

Watch a large building or skyscraper being taken down with explosive demolition. Be right there as the building crumples in on itself and falls straight down in a heap.

Build a Boat

Build your own boat. It can be a powerboat or a sailboat made out of wood or aluminum. It could be big enough for a day trip, a few overnights or an ocean voyage.

Finish the New York Times Sunday Crossword

Solve all the clues of a Sunday NYTs crossword puzzle.

Discover a New Species

You would figure that every species has been discovered, but every year a new living specimen or a fossil is found. Be an adventurer who goes where no one has gone before and you too could discover a new species.

Stay at a 5 Star Hotel

Reward yourself after you have completed one of your major goals by living like a high-rolling celebrity and staying at a 5 star hotel for a few days. Check out the spa while you're there.

Have Your Picture in the Paper

Maybe you're accepting an award, making a donation to charity with a big check or you got Timmy's dog out of the well.

Just make sure you get your picture in the paper for something good. Being arrested or doing something in public you shouldn't be doing doesn't cut it.

Be the First to Colonize a Distant Planet

This one may take a while, but at some point there will be a colony of humans on another planet. The moon or Mars seem most likely.

Ride a Steam Train

Take a day trip or a week-long adventure on a steam train. Head through the mountains and over a trestle (look out below!).

Quit Drinking

If you are a problem drinker, seek help and learn to live without alcohol.

Even if you don't abuse alcohol, try giving it up for a while. Your liver will thank you and you may lose a few pounds from not consuming so many empty calories.

Go to the Burning Man Festival

Head out to the Black Rock Desert in Nevada and watch a large wooden effigy go up in flames.

Go there in your art car to celebrate self-expression and self-reliance.

Ride the Top 10 Roller Coasters

You can start with the top ten in your own country then go for the top ten in the world. Scream down a run at over 120 miles per hour on a metal beast or wooden stomach turner. This list can be subjective and may change over time.

Take Up a Martial Art

You can learn Karate, Judo, Jujutsu, Aikido, Kendo and any of the martial arts you are interested in.

Most places will allow you to try a free class first to see if you are interested in going further.

Take Up a New Sport
Tennis, darts, Formula One racing, softball, bowling, biking or any other sport you have always wanted to try.

Climb the Seven Summits
Climb the highest peaks of the seven continents: Everest in Nepal, Kilimanjaro in Tanzania, Aconcagua in Argentina, Elbrus in Georgia, Carstensz Pyramid in Indonesia, Vinson Massif in Antarctica and McKinley in Alaska.

Pack a lunch.

Quit Over-Eating
Try eating two pieces of pizza and a salad instead of the whole pie, a scoop if ice cream instead of the container and a couple of cookies or potato chips instead of the entire bag.

Wait twenty minutes before going for that second helping at dinner.

Take a Cruise on the Queen Mary
Enjoy a cruise on one of the most magnificent ocean liners ever built. Travel to the Mediterranean, Scandinavia or around the world.

Ride a Camel in the Desert
A camel can spit, be bad-tempered and will most likely make your bag of sports equipment smell good.

Make sure you go with a reputable tour group and negotiate the price before you get on.

Go Tubing at a Water Park
Tubing at a water park is a great way to have fun and to beat the summer heat at the same time.

See an Active Volcano
Watch an eruption of Mount Etna in Italy or Kilauea in Hawaii. Bring marshmallows.

Enter a Bonspiel
Join your local curling club and learn the game. It's like shuffle board on ice with stranger terminology. Then get on a team and go to a bonspiel (tournament).

Travel One Long National Trail
You can bike, hike, or walk a trail that can take you through some of the most beautiful countryside in the world.

How about the 2,100-mile Appalachian Trail or the North Country Trail's 4400 miles if you have a little more time?

Go to the Four Major Golf Championships
See the Masters Golf Tournament in Augusta, Georgia, the US Open, the British Open and the PGA Championship.

Rent a Houseboat
Rent a houseboat for a relaxing, week-long cruise around a river system or lake. Barbeque, swim and work on your tan.

Compete in a Body Building Competition
Pump that iron until you're pumped and maintain a strict diet until you're ripped, then enter a body building competition.

See a Broadway Play
Catch a Broadway musical or a play in New York.

Write a Song or Poem
Let your heart pour out the words to a song or poem of your own creation. Dedicate it to the love of your life or your dog.

Explore a National Park
Go for a hike or a paddle for an afternoon, or sleep out under the stars for a week or more at a National Park.

Raise Money for a Charity
Collect donations and run or walk to raise money for a charity.

Bull Running in Spain
See or participate in the running of the bulls in Pamplona, Spain.

Have a Baby
You and your spouse can have a child together if you are ready and want to. The average cost of bringing up a child to 18 years old today is ten times your current salary, minus $2.

Adopt a Child
Give your love to a child who needs parents.

See the Dalai Lama Speak
Find out the nearest place to you where the Dalai Lama is speaking and go see him.

Soak in a Hot Spring
On your next vacation, go to a place that has a local hot spring and go for a soak.

Make a Medical Discovery

Discover a cure for a disease or the common cold, regenerate limbs, repair spinal cords or cure baldness.

Remember People's Names

Practice remembering the names of people you just met. Use it in a sentence as soon as you can to help you remember.

Take a Cross Country RV Trip

Buy or rent an RV and hit the open road for an entire summer.

Watch a Space Flight Launch

Head out to the launch pad visitor's gallery and watch in person as a rocket blasts off into space.

See the Northern Lights

Head up north far enough to get a good view of the northern lights or aurora borealis. The sky will put on a light show as particles from the sun interact with the earth's upper atmosphere. Book your spot in the Yukon for next year.

Learn a New Language

You could learn French, Spanish, Mandarin or any other language that interests you. Pig Latin doesn't count.

Create a Successful Ecommerce Web Site

Here is your chance to make a pile of money with your successful ecommerce web site.

Find or make a product, then set up a web site and perfect your SEO (search engine optimization) to drive people to your site.

Win a Grammy Award or an Oscar
Let your talent shine and you may be acknowledged as the best at your craft.

Know a Few Magic Tricks
Practice a few card tricks, some slight of hand and an illusion and you can use to break the ice at any party or event.

Bungee Jump off a Bridge
Tie yourself to a big elastic-like band and jump off a bridge over a river. You can do it naked at some sites.

Learn to Dance
Learn a few of the latest dance moves and a few classics like Ballroom, Salsa and the Tango, and you'll be ready for any occasion.

Sail in a Regatta
Enter your own boat or crew in a sailing regatta.

Discover a Totally New Energy Source
Use the force of gravity, magnetism or neutrinos to create massive amount of renewable energy.

Tell a Few Jokes
Memorize a dozen jokes on several different topics and learn how to tell them well.

Eat Organic Food
Eat organic food as much as possible. Try to eat local also, or better yet, grow your own.

Meet New People

Try new things and meet new people. Aim to meet ten new people a week.

Read the Top 100 Books

Search for a list of the top 100 books of all time. You may have to combine a couple to come up with your own list, and then head down to your local library and start reading.

Go on a Round-the-World Trip

You can take a cruise, bike, walk or ride a motorcycle around the world on a year-long adventure.

Have a Few Toasts Ready

Collect a few toasts that you can keep on the ready in case an event comes up where you will be required to say a few words.

Sail the Seven Seas

Sail the Adriatic Sea, the Caspian Sea, the Persian Gulf, the Black Sea, the Red Sea (and Dead Sea and Sea of Galilee), the Mediterranean Sea (including the Aegean Sea) and the Arabian Sea (part of the Indian Ocean).

Walk in a Forest Canopy

Walk along a catwalk that is suspended near the tree tops in a forest. Click your safety line to the steel cable and go for a stroll that offers a birds-eye view.

See a Professional Sporting Event

Get tickets and go and see a professional hockey, football, baseball and basketball game each year.

Learn to Weld
There is always a need to weld or solder something together, and if you can do it yourself and you can save having to hire someone.

Fly a Jet Fighter
You can fly a Russian MiG-29 jet fighter over the Russian countryside or a Buccaneer over South Africa.

Reduce Recreational Drug Use
Many people only do drugs because their own lives are dull and boring. Create an awesome list of things to do to make your life exciting that doesn't include drugs.

Be on Radio or TV
Have something newsworthy to tell people and your local radio or TV station might make you a star. Make the most of your 15 minutes of fame.

Fly First Class
Upgrade your tickets to a first class seat the next time you go on a long haul flight and enjoy the good life. You get a warm towel (no bathing), free dish of peanuts (don't fill your pockets) and free drinks (don't fill your wineskin).

Try Hang Gliding
Strap yourself to the underside of a triangular kite and jump off a hillside. Professional training is advised.

Take an Adventure Trip from Alaska to Argentina
Do an adventure trip from Alaska to Argentina by car, bike or foot power. Or pick an equally long journey of discovery.

Conclusion

By now your notebook has several pages of the things you want to have and the things you want to do. Your life is shaping up to become very exciting and it will help you become a very interesting person to know.

The best way to do some of the things on your list is to plan ahead. Pick a day and commit to it. Spontaneous adventures often don't work out or come about.

The next section will help you build the person you want to become.

———•◆•———

Chapter Three

Things to Be

Introduction

Go through this section to create a list of the qualities you want to develop in yourself. This will be the basis of creating the person you want to be.

Too many people mature to about age fifteen and then stop, changing very little over the course of their lives.

Every day brings with it an opportunity to grow and become a better, well-rounded and wonderful you.

Be More Forgiving

Forgive the driver who cut you off yesterday and the one from 18 years ago. Forgive your son for leaving his socks in the middle of the living room floor for the 4 billionth time. Forgive Mom and Dad for they did their best. Forgive yourself because it's O.K. not to be perfect.

Dwell on the Positive

Finding fault and complaining isn't an enjoyable way to spend your day. You don't have to be a Pollyanna, but looking for the positive in people and the day's events will make you a happier person.

Develop a Positive Attitude

This isn't a head-in-the-sand attitude, but a way of looking at life from a positive point of view rather than always looking for what is wrong. It just makes things easier.

Do No Harm

Treat others with kindness, whether it's an animal or a person. Deliberately treating others in a mean and spiteful way is a reflection of your poor opinion of yourself, as you can only build yourself up by tearing another down. Respect others, animals and the environment.

Practice Being Non-judgemental

Try to be open-minded to the viewpoint of other people. Accept people as they are without a critical attitude. Be aware of your thoughts and let them pass.

Practice this one while you're driving, standing in a line-up or reading the paper. Try to judge life less and enjoy it more.

Be Someone Who Lives Within Their Means

Try to make the money first and buy what you like when you can afford to do so. Going home with that new shiny bauble is so easy when you can whip out the plastic and charge it. Charge companies have done a great job conditioning us to be interest slaves.

More, bigger and better isn't always best for you. Things are not always what you want; it's how they are supposed to make you feel that attracts you. But the advertising is just smoke and mirrors. You'll soon tire of what you just bought and move on to something else.

Be a Happy Person
Choose to be happy. You may not like the situation you are in or the tasks you have to do, but being miserable won't change anything. Being happy will make life easier for you and those around you.

Move Forward in Spite of Fear
Everyone is afraid at some point but don't let it stop you from doing something you always wanted to try.

Be the Best Parent You Can Be
Be committed to continual learning in order to be skilled at all the issues that will come your way as a parent. Help your child reach their full potential with love, encouragement and guidance. Go with them to your local park and play on the swings or shoot some hoops.

Be Physically Fit
Tired of the space tire, flabby arms and a butt so big you have to wear an orange triangle on it? Start with a walk around the block every day and then slowly increase the distance. Get together with a friend or two for company and encouragement.

You can strength train by doing push-ups, crunches and squats. There's no equipment to buy and no gym membership needed.

Anywhere you start is O.K. Walk around one block, do two push-ups or join an exercise class. You are not in competition with anyone else.

Let Someone Else be Right

Letting someone else be right now and then will keep minor differences from developing into brouhaha. So they put on a sock and a shoe and a sock and a shoe instead of a sock and a sock and a shoe and a shoe. Peace is free. Get as much as you can.

Stop Procrastinating

People sometimes don't complete a task because they fear ridicule if it's not perfect. Well, it never will be perfect. Your poem can have a few words changed, the dog house you've built could have a nicer roof and, if given a chance, Leonardo da Vinci would have changed the Mona Lisa back to the full-mouth smile he originally painted.

So give it your best shot and be happy with that.

Increase Your Love

Without love, life is just a bowl of bran flakes. Good for you but bland. Get over your ego and let the real you hang out.

Hockey great Wayne Gretzky once said "You miss 100% of the shots you don't take." If you ask someone out and they turn you down, you're no worse off than before. They are the one who blew a chance to be with a really great person.

Practice love every day by accepting people as they are and treating others as you would like to be treated.

Experience Joy

See the humour when things go right and especially when they go wrong and maintain an inner happiness at all times. Expect good things and find happiness in your everyday tasks.

Be at Peace

Develop an inner sense of calmness and try to resolve any difference you may have with someone else without yelling, name calling or anger.

Think peaceful thoughts, speak peaceful words and you will be at peace.

Be a Person with Patience

If you're in a line-up and the person ahead is fumbling for exact change, take a deep breath and have a chuckle reading the tabloid headlines. Chill out at the red light and don't get bent out of shape because the driver in front of you isn't going fast enough – it will only stress you out.

Learn to be tolerant of others and stop trying to rule the universe (that job's taken). De-stress by giving yourself more time to get where you have to be. Red lights are the universe's way of telling you to take a break and to calm yourself.

Act in a Kind Way

Show kindness by being thoughtful of the needs of others and being pleasant in your interactions. Be gentle with other people, animals and yourself.

Be a Good Person

You can start by not doing bad things like stealing and lying. Pump up your good karma by helping someone when they need a hand or by volunteering for a charity. You should always speak in a polite manner, be honest and be a person everyone can trust.

Be Faithful

Be committed in your relationships with your mate, family and friends. You stick by them in good times and more so in the bad. Practice being faithful by being reliable and someone who can be trusted and believed.

Be Gentle

Practice your self-control by speaking and acting in a gentle manner with people and animals. Handle property carefully and treat others in a soft and considerate way.

Maintain Your Self-Control

Keep a level head in stressful situations.

Show Compassion

Be understanding of another person's misfortune.

Say Something Nice or Be Quiet

Tell people when they're terrific and leave the petty criticism for petty people.

Give People the Benefit of the Doubt

It's possible that what the person did was not done deliberately or with malice. They may have just made a mistake, so don't take it personally and move on.

Let Other People be Right

Let someone else be right now and then and save your arguing for something truly important.

Be a Big Thinker and a Bigger Doer

It takes just as much brain power to come up with a little idea as it does to come up with a big idea. The big idea may be more involved, but by breaking it down into manageable steps it can be done.

Be Aware of Those Around You

Be aware that there are other people in the universe other than yourself so don't stop after taking one step off the bus, at the bottom of an escalator, one step in the door, or in the middle of an aisle while trying to decide what it is you want.

Become Wealthy

The best way to help the poor is not to become one of them. Use your excess wealth for the better good by helping and giving to others.

Celebrate Your Successes

Did you exercise three times this week, stick to your diet or not have a drink or a smoke? Celebrate in a small way every week to keep yourself motivated.

Tell the Truth

It's just plain easier to do. Besides, you will always be found out and people will think less of you if you don't tell the truth.

Be a Person of Integrity

Do what's right even if it's difficult, mean what you say and honour your promises.

Live Life to the Fullest with No Regrets

If you look back on the year just passed and you didn't really do anything, then it's time for a change of direction. Try something new, do something you have never tried and step out of your comfort zone.

Try to Move Toward What You Want and Not Away from What You Fear

Bring more of what you want into your life without living in fear.

Love Yourself

This isn't an egoistical thing but something you have to do for your own well-being. Don't do anything to harm yourself, and be kind and forgiving toward yourself. Accept yourself for who you are and make the changes you want to make.

Take More Risks

Not reckless risks but try for that new job, start a business, write that book, ask that person out or try something new.

Make Loving Relationships a Priority

Develop and maintain family relationships and deep friendships. They don't just happen; you have to work at them.

Live in the Moment

Try not to spend your life in the past with regrets or in the future with worry, but be 100% involved in whatever you are doing whether it is reading, washing the dishes or playing with your child.

Find Out What Makes You Happy

Make sure you have a ready list of the things that make you happy and are good for you and do them more often. You can't be dependent on others to make you happy.

Develop Determination
Be determined to complete what you start no matter what problems my crop up. Many successes are just one more effort away.

Be Comfortable at Public Speaking
The only way to be good at speaking before a crowd is to practice. Tell a joke in front of a small group, prepare and lead a toast at the next occasion at the office or at a dinner party. Join a group and conquer this fear.

Be Calm and Relaxed
The best way to become calm and relaxed is to practice being calm and relaxed. If you can drive to and from work in rush hour traffic while maintaining your Zen-like bliss then, grasshopper, you have arrived.

Be a Life-Long Learner
Learning doesn't end after school but should continue your entire life. Be open and learn from those around you. Take a class or join a club.

Have an Attitude of Abundance
Realize that there is more than enough to go around and that a life of abundance is the way we were meant to live.

Use The Power of Positive Thinking
You attract what you think about. Try to keep thoughts of love, abundance and joy foremost in your mind. A self-defeated attitude will just get you more of the same, while thoughts of a better life will attract opportunity into your life.

Listen to Your Heart

You are going to fulfill your destiny. You have an ability within you that will bring you a life of excitement and fulfillment. You may not know what it is yet, but if you meditate to quiet your mind, your heart will point the way. Learn to listen to your heart.

Put Some Enthusiasm into Every Day

You may have a slower day now and again, but even then, take a look at one of the goals you are working on and develop enthusiasm for the rest of the day.

Realize that More Stuff Isn't Necessarily Better

After a point, owning more and more stuff isn't going to make your life better. It can drain your financial resources and clutter your life. If you're looking for enjoyment in things you will always be wanting for more and forever be disappointed.

Be a Nightly Reader

Spend 20-30 minutes or more each night reading for enjoyment.

Be a Giver, not a Taker

You can give a gift, a smile, a flower or some time. Taking and hoarding bottles up the energy flow of the universe.

Make a Difference Each Day

Smile at a the store clerk who helps you, recycle your soda can, toss some change in a street musician's hat, let a driver pull in front of you or anything else to make this place called Earth a better place because you are here.

Have Courage to Follow Your Heart

You can find meaning in life by following your heart and being true to your real self, not the phoney front you hide behind. Follow your true path and happiness will come.

See the Best in Everything

It's easy to be a life critic and whine about everything and everyone, but rise up above the petty and look for the good in situations and other people. Many disappointments hold the seed for greatness to come your way.

Leave a Legacy of Success and Abundance

Pave the way for others in your family line for a life of abundance and success so they can rise up even higher than you and make the lives of their children prosperous.

Make Getting Enough Sleep a Priority

Most people cut back on sleep in exchange for more time socializing, working or other activities. Then they drag the body through the next day fuelled with coffee and chocolate bars. They can be short-tempered, have foggy thinking and just be plain too tired for many activities.

Make getting sleep a high priority in your life. Put it right up there with exercise and eating healthy food.

Cleanliness is Your Natural State – Make it a Priority

Keep your clothes and body clean, pick up around your house, tidy up your yard and put that gum wrapper in your pocket until you are near a garbage can so you can throw it out properly rather than toss it on the ground. Organize a neighbourhood clean-up of an empty lot, an alley or a riverbank.

Make a Good First Impression

Be your best on a job interview and on a date, but also when you head out to the store. Don't wander out in track pants with your hair unwashed. You just may come across someone you really want to meet and if you're in slob mode it's probably not going to happen, or, if it does, it may go poorly.

Embrace Change

People want their lives to get better but they also want everything to stay the same. It can't happen. If you keep doing the same things you'll keep getting the same results.

Change can be successful when taken slowly and in steps. If you're overweight and out of shape you didn't get that way in the past 10 days and you won't see much improvement in the next 10 days, contrary to what TV advertisers of exercise equipment and diet systems will have you believe.

Be a Wonderful Listener

Focus in on what a person is saying to you and resist the urge to cut them off and jump in with a 'me too' story of your own. Let the other person take the spotlight and just ask some questions relevant to what they are talking about. You'll soon get a reputation as a great person to talk to and you'll learn a lot about other people too.

Treat Sales People and Servers with Respect

Don't yell at a sales clerk because you can find what you are looking for or if the item is out of stock. They don't order the merchandise or control the delivery. People serving your food are also not there to instantly respond to your snapping fingers.

Expect Good Things to Happen to You

Good things may come your way if you're expecting them but if you're always expecting the worse, you also won't be disappointed. Life is a collection of choices so why not expect the best?

Seek More Responsibility

Ask you boss for more responsibility at work and you may find yourself getting an unexpected raise. If you just show up and do the bare minimum you could also find yourself first in line when a layoff comes.

Maintain a Sense of Humour

You'll just be more pleasant to be around. It will also make the day more enjoyable and you'll feel better about yourself and others.

Be Reliable

Be a person others can count on. If you say you are going to be at a certain place at a certain time then be there on time. If you say you are going to do something by a certain time, then get it done on time, if not earlier.

Make you word your bond. Others may let you down and keep you waiting, but you're a person others can count on. Be a person of your word.

Take Responsibility for Your Actions and Thoughts

If you did something wrong, own up and try to make amends. If you're late for work, don't blame the weather or the traffic when you didn't leave enough time to get where you had to be.

Everyone makes mistakes so don't try to hide them or find someone else to blame them on. Cowboy it up and make things right if you can. Say you're sorry, repay the money you borrowed or help fix the fence you damaged.

Be Flexible

Sometimes you have to change your plans because an unexpected event came up. It would be great if everything always worked out as it was supposed to, but have a plan 'B' already thought out and in your back pocket if you need it.

Be Appreciative and Grateful

Take a few moments at the end of your day to be appreciative and grateful for what happened during the day. Don't dwell on whatever didn't work out but be thankful for the people in your life and the events that made your day a great experience.

You can also write your appreciative and grateful thoughts down in a journal every night. Make a point of listing five things every day you are grateful for. On a day you are especially down and discouraged, read through entries of previous days to lighten your spirit, and then write down five entries for that discouraging day. Finding five positive things you can be grateful for, no matter how small, can make you feel a lot better.

Everything in Moderation

Food, drink, physical activities and even emotions are all O.K. if not done to excess.

Look for Opportunities in Problem Situations
Finding fault and someone to blame is easy but it will accomplished nothing. Realize that you are probably not the only person to experience the problem. There could be a new product or service that you could develop to solve the issue.

Be Generous with Hugs and Smiles
They're both free and you and the recipient will feel better. Hug your child, your mate or your pet. Smile at the mail person, the cashier or the person you pass on the sidewalk.

Be Willing to Help a Stranger
It could be as simple as phoning for help, assisting someone who has dropped a bag of groceries or holding a door open for a person behind you at the mall.

Do One Small Thing Every Day
Make yourself and the world a better place by doing one small thing every day. You could pick up a piece of trash on your walk and throw it in the next garbage container, clean off your desk or talk to your neighbour for a few minutes.

Be Polite
It doesn't take any longer than being rude, it's free and other people will appreciate your thoughtfulness.

Develop Determination
Blast though any roadblocks stopping you from completing a task with unwavering determination. Exercise every day so you can lose that weight, write or read for one hour every day so you can finish your book or keep on working toward your degree.

Eliminate Self-Limiting Beliefs

Shut down that voice in your head that says you're not smart enough, or young enough or strong enough. There is always a way so quiet your mind and let the answer come to you.

Charge Up Your "How are you?" Answer

If your answer is a stock "Fine" or "O.K." then easily make yourself and those around you feel better by responding with any of the following (or one of your own): fabulous, dynamite, incredible, unbelievably blessed, jazzed, cosmic, awesome or righteous.

Be Optimistic About Your Future

You don't have to be unrealistic, but every day is a choice so why choose to be negative and miserable? It's not going to help your situation and you're just going to bring down everyone you come in contact with.

Have Respect for Others

Have respect for other people, other creatures, other cultures and other ways of thinking. If you were always right then you would be ruler of the universe, but since that job is already taken, relax and let things be.

Accept That the Past is Over and Done

Focus on where you want to go, not where you have been. If you make a mistake or miss an opportunity, let it go and move on. Just as the wake behind a boat doesn't control where the boat goes next, your past should not control where you go and what you do today.

Be One of the Best Drivers in the World

You may make a mistake now and again but you can still be one of the best car drivers in the world by developing one skill. That is the ability to make any kind of left turn and stay on your own side of the road. You can realize that you don't have to drive three feet over the centre line because your lane is the same size all the way around.

Read Empowering Books

Read self-improvement books, autobiographies of successful people and stories of people who have overcome obstacles to fulfill their dreams. Even a few pages a night will make a big difference in your outlook.

Be Generous

Freely give away your love, time for your family and friends and even some of your possessions. Give without expecting anything in return. If you have some extra, give some to a person who is lacking. The funny thing about giving is that you can throw out a one pound boomerang of giving and it will come back into your life from a completely different direction now weighing ten pounds. What goes out comes back multiplied.

Create Your Own Lifestyle

The best way to produce a lifestyle you would like is to do what you enjoy. You could make more money at another job, but if at the end if the day you are exhausted, despondent and you hate doing what you do, then it just isn't worth it. If you do what you enjoy you will be good at it and you will be happier and more prosperous.

Try Your Best

Many people fail at something they try, not because of a lack of skill or ability, but because they quit without really giving the task much of an effort. If you tried your best and failed you can still be proud of your effort and maybe you'll do better next time.

Don't Fret Feedback

If someone comments on your work or something that you have done, don't take it personally and be defensive. Use what they have said as a way to improve.

Be an Expert in Your Field

If you read just one book each week on a subject related to your field of interest, in just a few years you could be an expert in that field. At the least you will have amassed enough knowledge to be the "go to" person where you work, be a more valuable employee and make more money.

Give Compliments Freely

If someone you meet is dressed nicely, tell them so. Did they give a great presentation or do something nice for someone else? Then let them know. People love to be recognized.

Enjoy the Journey and the Destination

It's natural to be excited about arriving at your destination but notice what's going on around you during the journey. This can be a car or plane trip but also a project you're working on.

Give and Save Ten Percent

Give 10 percent of what you make to a local charity and save 10 percent of every dollar you make (and never spend it). Your local charity can make better use of your donation than the government and the money you save is your golden goose - so don't kill it.

Be Proactive

Try to anticipate a problem and correct the situation as soon as you can, or fix a problem before someone tells you to.

Have a Plan 'B' Ready

It would be great if all our plans worked out but sometimes you'll have to change them when they go wrong so be prepared. Do you know several ways to get to work if your regular route is blocked by traffic or construction?

Eat More Vegetarian Meals

Give your arteries a break and load up with all the nutrients that vegetables are packed with. It can also be less expensive and trying new meals keeps you from the rut of eating the same foods every day.

Recycle, Reuse and Reduce

It's the right thing to do.

Live Your Dreams

Live your life journey the way you want, doing the things you want, when you want. Just keep it fun and don't harm anyone. Find your joy and passion and live your life around it.

Be Loyal

Be someone other people can count on and trust. Stick by your friends and family and respect the relationships you have.

Control Your Feelings to Control Your Destiny

Vocalizing every thought is not always a good thing, nor is acting on every impulse. Screaming at a two-year-old, pushing the cop who gave you a ticket or stealing something because you thought no one was looking will result in bigger problems than those caused by the original situation.

Speak Up at the Right Moment

Learn to be assertive in order to speak up when something isn't right or you are being treated poorly. Don't stand for abuse, call 911 when your friend drives off extremely drunk or tell a bully to back off.

Work on Yourself

Spend the time to work on yourself in order to become a better person, happier with whom you are and someone other people look up to. If you want something in your life to change, then you have to start by changing yourself.

Spend Some Time in Reflection

Take a few minutes at the end of the day to think about what you accomplished and to give yourself a pat on the back and make note of things you could have done better. Write all your accomplishments down in a journal.

Spend a little more time and review your top goals weekly and make any adjustments if you got off track. Take a little longer at the end of the year to read through your journal and be proud of your accomplishments.

Develop Sportsmanship

You could cheat at a game and win but realize that the only reason you did cheat was because you were afraid you were going to lose. If you tried your best and lost, you have nothing to feel bad about, but if you only won by cheating then the only person you really hurt was yourself.

Play by the rules, be graceful if you lose and humble when you win.

Be a Mentor

If someone helped you learn something (or even if no one did) give back by being a mentor and teach someone else what you have learned.

Conclusion

The biggest hindrance to your potential will come from the limits you place upon yourself. So remove or blast through any self-limiting beliefs you have.

Be a better you than the person you were last year and go further next year from where you are today.

I hope you have added dozens of items from this section to your list of the things you want to be.

Changing as a person can be difficult, time-consuming and often frustrating. Don't try to change forty things at once because it will be impossible. Pick the one that would give you the most bang for your buck if you made it part of your life. Master that one item first, and then start on another one.

You know what is most important and what could drastically improve the quality of your life. Take one step at a time and ask for help if you need it.

Things That Make You Feel Good

Introduction

One of the reasons some people slip into abusing alcohol and drugs is that these substances are an easy way to change the way they are feeling. Unfortunately, making changes in this way are often destructive to their health, their interpersonal relationships and they are just a temporary escape from the problems of their lives.

Your aim in this section is to come up with a list of things you can do that will make you feel better and that are good for you.

You are going to have problems in your life. Some days you are going to feel down, sad and dejected. This is perfectly normal and it is something that can't be avoided.

What you can do is prepare ahead of these bad times with a grab bag of things you can do to change your mood and uplift your spirits without causing any adverse effects in your life.

Unless you are suffering from clinical depression, most sad feelings you have will be temporary and are often over within a day or two.

Create your own, personalized list of ways you can change your mood for the better and come out of the blues feeling stronger and more optimistic than ever before.

A Walk in the Woods

Enjoy a walk during the fall with the crisp air and the crunch of leaves underfoot, or during the summer with the smell of the pine trees. Be at one with nature and have a leisurely stroll by yourself or with your family.

Enjoy a Hot Cup of Coffee or Tea

Take a time out, sit down and relax with your favourite hot beverage. The aroma of a fresh brew is divine. Sit outside on your deck early in the morning.

Watch a Sunset

Find a spot on a hill or by the water and watch in awe as the sun disappears below the horizon. From golden to deep purple it's a sight that should be enjoyed at least once a month.

Listen to Music

Easy listening, country, classical, rock and roll or polka music can fill your heart with joy, reduce stress and give you an emotional, natural high.

Take a Bubble Bath

Turn off the phone, shut the door and hang a "Do Not Disturb" sign on the knob. Light a few candles, put some music on and then slip into a hot bubble bath. Put in more hot water using just your toes.

Have a Round of Golf with a Cart
You usually walk the course, but once in awhile get a cart and enjoy the ride.

Go for a Bike Ride
Strap on your helmet and get peddling. You can experience some fresh air and exercise and maybe lose a few pounds to boot. Drive single file on the right-hand side of the road or along a bike path and remember to bring a water bottle.

Walk Barefoot
Take off your shoes and enjoy the soft grass between your toes.

Sit by the Water
Just sit there and watch the waves on the ocean, the peaceful surface of a lake or the flow of a river. The rhythms of the water can be calming.

Go to the Wave Pool
Grab the kids and your water wings and spend a few hours just being silly. Go down the water slide, then grab hold of a foam mat, head to the deep end and hold on for the big one. Take a break in the sauna or hot tub.

Go on a Picnic
Pack a basket with some cold fried chicken, potato salad and fresh bread and go to a park for a picnic. Lay down your blanket and just relax.

Sit by a Fire

You can sit by a campfire or in front of your fireplace. Stir up the fire, add another log and then be mesmerized by the dancing of the flames.

Give Some Hugs

Hug your mate, child, pet or your boss. Be careful with that last one.

Go for a Run

Go for a run early in the morning before most other people are out of bed or in the early evening as the day is quieting down.

Bake Some Chocolate Chip Cookies

The aroma of homemade, freshly-baked chocolate chip cookies gets your mouth salivating. Test out a few while they are still toasty.

Watch TV

Curl up on your couch and watch your favourite TV show.

Walk on the Beach

Feel the sand between your toes and listen to the waves lapping the shore. Maybe you have your boots and jacket on as a winter storm approaches.

Look at the Clouds

Find a wide open patch of grass and lay back and look up at the fluffy clouds above. What images can you see?

Date Night

Get out and meet someone new or set aside one night a week to be with your mate. Get a sitter for the kids if you have to but make some time for yourselves.

Go for a Drive

Even with the price of gas, five to ten dollars can get you pretty far. Drive down a back country road, through a forested area or along the coast on a sunny afternoon.

Blow Some Bubbles

Mix up a batch of homemade bubble solution and pick up some dollar store wands and make some bubbles. The kids love it and so does Grandma.

Skip Rope

Remember back when you could skip rope all afternoon? Now you can barely do it for 12 seconds before you fumble up or are out of breath. Let your kids show you how it's done.

Take Your Child to the Park

Sit back on a bench and watch your child play in the park.

Walk Your Dog

Head out to the off-leash area and let your dog run and play with other dogs or go for a walk around your neighbourhood.

Bake Something

You can't go wrong with baking a cake, pie or some brownies. How about some fresh baked bread or rolls for dinner tonight?

Go to the Movies

Go see the latest blockbuster movie or an indie flick no one has heard of.

Go Fly a Kite

Enjoy some fresh air and see how high you can get your kite to soar.

Look up at the Stars

Pick a moonless night and go outside in the evening and look up at the stars. Pick up a book on the constellations from your local library and see how many you can find.

Play a Round of Pitch and Putt

It's a great way to work on your short game. Bring a few short clubs and your putter and play a round in and hour or so.

Take an Evening Walk after a Snowfall

Put on you coat and boots and walk down a quiet street after a fresh snowfall.

Make a Scrapbook

Work on putting together a scrapbook from that old box of photographs so you can preserve your family history. Add some movie or show ticket stubs, a ribbon that was won in a race and some quotes from family members.

Make Something in Your Workshop/Craft Room

Indulge in your hobby. Build a jewellery box for that special someone's birthday or some shelving for the laundry room to clean up the clutter.

You could knit a sweater, make a quilt, paint a picture or create some pottery.

Start a Book Club or Wine Appreciation Group
Share your love of reading great books or enjoying wine by starting your own group.

Pet Your Animal
Give your cat or dog a good belly rub and a head scratching. Their unconditional love will take away the blues.

Go for an Afternoon Nap
Slide a lounge chair into the shade, slip into your hammock or curl up on the couch for a little snooze.

Write in Your Diary
Record your thoughts and what you are feeling in a diary or journal.

Call a Friend You Haven't Heard from in Awhile
Let them know you were thinking about them and wanted to catch up on what was happening in their life.

Enjoy Some Dark Chocolate
Fine, dark chocolate can be an antioxidant and can lower your blood pressure. But enjoy it just because it tastes so good.

Rent a Movie
Pick up a few movies you have wanted to see, pop up a big bowl of popcorn and turn off the lights. You can pause the movie when you have to go to the bathroom and there is no one behind you talking. And hopefully your floor isn't sticky.

Cut the Grass
Enjoy the smell of a freshly cut lawn.

Go to a Spa
Pamper yourself for a few hours or an entire day at a spa.

Play a Round of Mini Putt
Play a round of mint putt and then go for ice cream afterwards.

Play with Your Kid (or as a Kid)
Go out and toss the ball around, shoot some hoops or play hopscotch.

Surf the Web
Check out your social networking sites, look up something you want to know about or Google yourself.

Clean out a Closet
Maybe not something you want to do on a regular basis, but if it was one of those jobs you have been putting off, getting it done will feel great. Do only one shelf at a time, then take a break.

Go Kayaking
Paddle around the island or bay for the afternoon.

Enjoy an Iced Tea on a Hot Afternoon
Enjoy a tall glass of iced tea on a hot summer afternoon. Take a glass or mug out of your freezer for the best results.

Exercise
Lift weights, swim, do yoga or join a spin class. The endorphins from exercising are a natural high.

Have your House Cleaned

Hire a house cleaning service and take off for the day. When you come home to a clean, fresh house it will feel fantastic. Enjoy it. It may only last a few days.

Call in Sick

Not something to do on a regular basis, but once in a while call in sick and spend the day downtown doing whatever you want.

Yoga

Take some time for yourself and do some yoga or pilates.

Sleep in Late

When the weekend rolls around, take a dark, rainy Sunday morning and just stay in bed until noon.

Look at Old Photographs

Take out an album of your photographs and flip through it remembering the great times of your life.

Meditate

Build up your meditation sessions to 20 minutes, twice a day, to relieve stress and for self transformation.

Take a Day of Rest

Sunday used to be the day of rest, but with everyone's busy lives we're going seven days a week. But now and again, take Sunday off and just relax without doing any chores, working or paying bills.

Get a Massage
Reward yourself for a project you completed by treating yourself to a massage. You can have just your back done, just your feet, or you can go for an entire body massage.

Go Fishing
A lot of times catching a fish is a bonus. It's just relaxing to be out on or by the water away from the busyness of your life.

Take a Long Shower
Wash off the worries of the day with a leisurely, hot shower.

Buy a New Pair of Shoes
Take an afternoon and go browsing for a new pair of shoes.

Listen to an Empowering Program
There are many life-affirming, soul-energizing and motivational audio programs you can listen to. You can learn something new, reinforce something you already know or recharge your batteries.

Read a Book
Read the latest book by your favourite author.

Make a Sandcastle or a Snowman
Get out of the house and enjoy the day by building a sandcastle or a snowman. It can be as simple or as complex as you like because there are no rules.

Get Away for a 3-Day Weekend
Take advantage of a holiday that falls on a Friday or Monday and take off for a 3-day getaway. You can go sit on a beach in the sun or visit a friend.

Sit in the Sauna

A lot of swimming complexes have a sauna. For only a few dollars, enjoy a sauna then jump into the pool for a quick cool down.

Play in the Rain

Put on your boots and raincoat and go for a walk in the rain. If you come across a puddle that needs splashing in, go for it.

Go to a Baseball, Football or Hockey Game

You can go to a professional game or support your local college or high school team.

Go to the Park

Bring along a kid or just be one yourself and go for a swing, a slide or sit on the teeter totter.

Skinny Dip at Night

Sneak out to your pool in the evening for a swim sans bathing suit.

Play a Card or Board Game

Play cards or get out a board game for a TV-free couple of hours.

Conclusion

Now you are prepared with a host of ways to make yourself feel better in ways that are good for you.

Life may knock you down but you have the strength to overcome any obstacle that may come your way.

But why wait? Try to include any of the items from this list (or your own) into your life either daily, weekly or once a month.

Chapter Five

Jobs to Have

Introduction

Now is the time to put some thought into how you are going to pay for the things you want and the things you want to do. But, more importantly, this is how you will be spending most of your time every day.

Keep a few things in mind. The ideal situation is to find a career that involves something you enjoy doing and are good at and that someone will pay you to do. Realize that you can get what you want in life if you help others get what they want.

You should also consider a career that can't be outsourced. There is no such thing as an overseas plumber or dental hygienist. Find a career that requires your physical presence like a hair stylist or an actor.

Some areas of growth will be in health care for baby boomers: everything from doctors, optometrists and social assistance specialists to veterinarians. You also need to have the courage to drop an idea you have if you find that in a few years' time employment will decrease in that field or the job may disappear entirely.

Trades will be in demand like plumbers, electricians and various fields in construction. Anything in the green field will explode like energy experts who know how to save energy as well as experts in renewable or alternative energies.

If you don't know what you want to do, ask yourself what you're good at and what sort of activities you enjoy. Then browse through the following list of suggestions and see if anything catches your interest or fits with something you're passionate about.

This section is the longest, but the job titles and descriptions are short and to the point so you should be able to cover it quickly. You should be able to tell if you are interested or not in the job listing right away. Go with your gut feeling.

When you get to the end of this job section, you should have ten to twenty possibilities written down that you can investigate further.

Abandoned Mine Plugger
Cover up mines and wells that are no longer used.

Academic Dean
Be the leader of a department at a college or university.

Accordionist
You play a portable squeeze box.

Account Executive
A sales representative in charge of customer accounts.

Accountant
Keep financial records for a company.

Accounting Clerk
Record accounts payable and receivable.

Acoustical Carpenter
Build sound-absorbing rooms.

Acrobat
Perform dance and gymnastic feats in a circus.

Actor
Play a role on stage, TV or radio.

Actuary
Estimate risk and uncertainty in the insurance field.

Administrative Assistant/Clerk
Perform secretarial duties in an office.

Administrative Service Manager
Coordinate many support services for a company.

Admissions Officer
Process student applications at a school.

Admitting Clerk
Enter patient information for admission to a hospital.

Adventure Guide
Lead people on outdoor adventure tours.

Adventurer
Someone who climbs mountains, flies planes and does many other outdoor activities.

Advertising Sales Agent
Sell ads in papers, magazines, radio and TV.

Advocate
Stand up for another for a cause.

Aerobics Instructor
Work at a health club leading a class in exercises set to music.

Aeronautical Engineer
Work to design and construct of aircraft.

Aerospace engineer
Work to design and construct aircraft and space craft.

Aesthetician
Give people beauty treatments.

Agent (Artist, Performer, Athlete)
Represent a performer or athlete in salary negotiations with team owners.

Agent (Spy)
Work covertly for the government watching the activities of another country.

Aggregate Plant Operator
Make big rocks into little rocks for construction projects and roadways.

Agricultural Equipment Technician
Repair and maintain farm equipment.

Agricultural Inspector
Inspect farms and processing plants to ensure businesses are complying with regulations.

Agricultural Scientist
Study and understand the practices used in agriculture.

Agricultural Worker
Work on farms planting, harvesting and tending to crops, and doing many other farm-related duties.

Agricultural and Food Scientist
Study ways to improve farming practices.

Agronomist
Find ways to use plants for fuel, food and fibre.

Aircraft Structural Technician
Build and repair planes.

Air Traffic Controller
Work in a control tower at an airport to direct airplane traffic.

Airbrush Artist
Use an airbrush to paint cars, motorcycles, people or to create works of art.

Air-Conditioning Mechanic/Installer
Install, maintain and repair residential and commercial air conditioning units.

Aircraft and Avionics Equipment Mechanics/Service Technicians
Inspect and repair aircraft and avionics equipment.

Aircraft Cargo Handlers
Load and unload freight and baggage to and from planes.

Aircraft Electrician
Maintain and repair electrical systems in aircraft.

Aircraft Engineer
Direct the maintenance and repair of planes and helicopters.

Aircraft Maintenance Technician/Mechanic
Perform maintenance and repair of planes and helicopters.

Aircraft Pilot/Co-pilot
Fly planes and helicopters.

Airfield Operations Specialist
Responsible for the safe takeoff and landing of aircraft.

Air Force
A branch of the military involved in aerial warfare.

Airman
Be a pilot or a crew member in the air force.

Album Cover Artist
Design artwork for music album and CD covers.

Alderman
A member of a municipal council who represents wards in their voting district.

Allergist
A physician trained to treat allergies and asthma.

Alligator Wrestler
Capture alligators to be removed from residential areas or for entertainment.

Ambassador
The highest ranking diplomat who represents their country in a foreign capital.

Ambulance Attendant/Paramedic
Provide emergency care to accident victims.

Ambulance Driver
Transport accident victims to a hospital.

Amusement Attendant
Work at carnivals, tourist attractions and theme parks selling tickets and operating rides.

Anaesthesiologist
A doctor who administers drugs to anesthetise a patient during surgery.

Animal Breeder
Select and breed animals for specific characteristics.

Animal Care Worker
Work at a kennel, shelter, farm or zoo feeding, grooming and caring for animals.

Animal Control Officer
Work for a city or town enforcing animal regulations, investigating animal cruelty complaints and educating the public on proper animal care.

Animal Food Maker
A person who makes, mixes and prepares food for animals at a factory or as a small scale operation.

Animal Renderer
Process animal by-products into useful materials like lard or tallow.

Animal Trainer
Train animals for the circus, zoos or at obedience schools.

Animator
An artist who draws images in frames to create the illusion of movement in movies, TV and games.

Announcer
An actor who does voice work for TV, movies and radio.

Anthropologist
Study the social and cultural characteristics of different cultures.

Antique Dealer
Buy and sell older furniture and collectables.

Apartment Manager
Rent out units, perform routine maintenance and collect rent.

Apparel Maker
Make clothing for the fashion industry.

Appliance Service Technician
Repair small appliances like toasters and microwaves or large appliances like refrigerators, stoves and washers.

Appraiser (jewellery, houses, cars, art)
Place a dollar value on a piece of property.

Aquarium Cleaner
Clean residential or commercial fish tanks.

Arboriculture (Urban Forestry)
Selection and care of trees in public spaces and parks.

Arborist
Care for ornamental trees.

Archaeologist
Examine artifacts from past cultures to learn about who they were and how they lived.

Archbishop
A leader of Christian diocese.

Archer
Someone who is an expert using the bow and arrow.

Architect
Design buildings and other construction projects.

Architectural Sheet Metal Worker
Work with metal to make and install gutters, flashing and more in the construction of buildings.

Archivist
Arrange, catalogue and store documents of value.

Armourer
Make and repair metal armour or small arms and weapons.

Army
Land-based military force. There are various roles for soldiers.

Aromatherapist
Use essential oils and other plant compounds to improve a person's mood or health.

Art Dealer
Buy and sell works of art like paintings or sculptures.

Art Director
Envision and direct the creation of art or scenes for movies, plays, TV and video games.

Art Therapist
A mental health discipline in which a therapist uses paint or markers to help people through traumas or mental illness.

Artificial Inseminator
Breed animal by manually injecting bull semen into cows.

Artisan
A skilled artist who hand makes household items, jewellery or furniture.

Artist
Create art using paint, sculpture or music.

Asphalt Paving Machine Operator
Control heavy equipment in the manufacture of roadways.

Asphalt Paving/Laydown Technician
Use heavy equipment to put down and smooth roadways.

Asphalt Plant Operator
Work at a plant that makes asphalt for paving.

Assayer
Analyze soil samples for mineral content and value.

Assembler/Fabricator
Make parts and finished products at a manufacturing site.

Assessor
Measure the value of buildings, machinery or property.

Astrologer
Use a horoscope to chart events in a person's life.

Astronaut
Pilot or act as crew of a space craft.

Astronomer
A scientist who studies stars, planets and galaxies.

Athlete
A person who practices a sport (eg. baseball player, hockey player, golfer, bowler).

Athletic Director
Oversee the athletic department of a school or professional sports club.

Athletic Trainer
Treat and help prevent sports injuries.

ATM Technician
Repair and maintain automatic teller machines.

Atmospheric Scientist
Study weather systems and the atmosphere around the earth and other planets.

Attorney
A lawyer who represents clients in the legal system.

Auctioneer
Control the bidding of items at a sale.

Audio Engineer
Work in a recording studio to enhance music.

Audiologist
An ear and hearing doctor.

Audio-Visual Collections Specialist
In charge of audio and visual equipment at a school.

Auditor
Review the accounting books of a company.

Automatic Transmission Service Technician
Repair and maintain the transmissions of cars and trucks.

Automobile Mechanic/Service Technician
Repair and maintain the mechanical parts of cars and trucks.

Automotive Body Repair
Work in a collision shop to repair body panels of cars and trucks.

Automotive Glass Technician
Repair and replace windows in vehicles.

Automotive Machinist
Make parts and repair or rebuild engines.

Automotive Painter
Work in a collision shop to repaint body panels of cars and trucks.

Automotive Radiator Manufacturer and Repairer
Test, repair and rebuild radiators in cars and trucks.

Automotive Refinishing Prep Technician
Clean, sand and prepare body panel parts for painting.

Automotive Upholsterer
Repair and rebuild seats in vehicles.

Automotive Wheel Alignment and Brake Service Technician
Check, align and repair braking systems on cars and trucks.

Avionics Technician
Repair and maintain the communications and navigation equipment on an aircraft.

Ayurvedic Healer
An alternative medical healer based in the traditional Hindu science of treating the mind, body and spirit as one.

Babysitter
Take care of another person's child for a few hours.

Backhoe Operator
Operate a heavy piece of construction equipment used for digging trenches and moving earth.

Baggage Porter
Work in hotels or airports carrying travellers' luggage.

Bagger
Work at a supermarket putting groceries into bags for customers.

Bailiff
Act as a guard in a courtroom.

Baker
Make breads, cakes and other baked goods.

Ballet Dancer
Use dance to act out a story on stage.

Balloonist
Fly a hot air or gas balloon on air currents. Can take passengers or be a commercial balloon.

Bank Teller
Work at a bank helping customers with their transactions.

Banquet Manager
Work at a hotel or conference centre catering to a business group, wedding or general meeting by providing food and refreshments.

Bar Manager
Work at a nightclub or restaurant managing employees, ordering supplies and serving alcoholic beverages.

Barber
Cut hair and shave or trim beards.

Barista
Prepare various coffee beverages.

Bartender
Work behind a counter (the bar) and serve alcoholic drinks in a nightclub or restaurant.

Basket Weaver
Bend materials like straw, grasses or wood into a basket shape.

Bassist
Play a bass guitar, tuba or other bass instrument.

Bathroom Attendant
Maintain the cleanliness of a public bathroom at a club or hotel and provide things like towels to customers.

Battery Repairer
Work at an automobile shop inspecting, repairing and replacing batteries in cars and trucks.

Beader
Make necklaces and bracelets by stringing beads together.

Beautician
Style hair and give cosmetic treatments in a beauty salon or for movies and TV.

Beauty Pageant Contestant
Enter competitions to be judged on beauty, talent and personality.

Bed and Breakfast Operator
Operate a large house where paying guests stay for short periods, usually just overnight.

Beekeeper

Tend bees in hives. Transport bees to fields for pollination, and extract honey and beeswax.

Beggar

Stand or sit on streets and corners asking people walking by for money.

Behavioural Interventionist

Assist families with programs designed to help children diagnosed with behavioural challenges.

Bellhop

Work at a hotel helping guest with their bags, deliver room service items and suggest local tourist attractions.

Benefits Administrator

Work at a company explaining employee benefits, tracking employee days off and overseeing health insurance claims.

Bicycle Mechanic

Assemble and repair bicycles at a store or shop.

Billboard Installer

Put up and change large advertising signs.

Bill Collector/Account Collector

Phone people who are behind in their debt payments and try to recover the amount due.

Bindery Operator

Use machines to assemble books with various kinds of binding methods.

Biochemist

Work in a lab as a scientist who studies chemical reactions and processes in living organisms for medical, agricultural or manufacturing organizations.

Biographer

An author who writes about the lives of other people.

Biologist

A scientist who studies how organisms work. May work in medicine, agriculture or industry.

Biomedical Engineer

Design artificial limbs, joints and valves by using engineering principles to solve healthcare problems.

Biometrician

Work to understand and expand human or animal life span.

Biophysicist

A scientist who studies how to apply physical principles to how organisms function.

Biostatistician

Apply statistics to biological experiments.

Birth Attendant

Help women during the birthing process. May also be known as a midwife or obstetrician.

Bishop

A spiritual leader of a diocese of the Christian clergy.

Blaster
Set up and detonate explosives at a construction or mining site.

Block Mason
Build walls, walkways and fences using stone or concrete blocks and bricks.

Blogger
A writer who posts short stories or articles to a web page.

Boat Operator
Drive a power boat for fishing charters, tourism or pleasure.

Boat Builder
Construct a boat with wood, fibreglass, metal or cement either at a shipyard or in a back shed. May also do repairs on boats.

Boatswain
Oversee a deck crew involved in loading and unloading, rigging or maintenance.

Body Double
Stand-in for an actor in dangerous or distance scenes in movies and TV.

Body Piercer
Put holes in various parts of a person's body for installing jewellery like earrings and studs. Often works with a tattoo artist.

Bodybuilder

Someone who lifts weights to build big muscles in order to enter contests or work at a health club.

Bodyguard

A person who protects their client from physical harm. Can work for entertainers, politicians or business people.

Boilermaker

A metal fabricator who builds and repairs boilers, furnaces and piping.

Bologna Maker

Make a tube of meat from low quality meat scraps.

Bomb Disposal Expert

Work in the army or the police department disarming explosive devices.

Bookbinder

Operate machines to make books.

Book Publisher

Have an author's work printed and available for sale.

Book Reviewer

Read a book and write an article stating your opinion of the book.

Booking Agent

Find jobs for entertainers like musicians and actors.

Bookkeeper

Record day-to-day accounting transactions.

Bookmobile Driver
Operate as a library on wheels and transport books and other material between branches.

Bookseller
Sell publisher's books to bookstores.

Book Shepherd
Someone who guides an author through creating and publishing a book.

Boom Truck Operator
Operate a boom crane that lifts construction material into place.

Border Patrol Agent
Watch a country's border for people trying to gain entry or smuggle goods into a country.

Botanist
A scientist interested in plants.

Bouncer/Doorman
Work at a nightclub providing security, controlling entry to the club and evicting unwanted guests.

Bounty Hunter
Someone who tracks down and captures fugitives for money.

Boxer
Fight in a ring.

Brace Maker
Make, fit and repair medical appliances like artificial limbs and braces.

Braille Clerk
Work in a library assisting sight impaired borrowers.

Brattice Builder
Build doors and ventilation walls in underground railway systems or mines.

Brewmaster
Responsible for making beer.

Bricklayer
Build walls, walkways and chimneys using bricks.

Bridge Tender/Lock Tender
Operate bridges and locks on canals to allow passage of vessels.

Bridge Worker
Repair and maintain bridges.

Broadcast Captioner
Provide instantaneous translation for closed-captioning on live television programs for the hearing impaired.

Broadcast Engineer
Involved in the transmission of TV and radio signals.

Brokerage Clerk
Work in the financial services industry in the trading of stocks, related paperwork and record keeping.

Bucker
Work in the logging industry using a chain saw to cut up felled trees.

Budget Analyst
Examine and develop budgets for the distribution of a company's financial resources.

Building Cleaner
A janitor who cleans an office building, mall or hotel.

Building Envelope Technician
Responsible for all aspects of exterior wall construction and repair.

Building Inspector
Ensure buildings are constructed and repaired according to safety code regulations.

Building Manager
Can be in charge of the operations related to a conference centre of hotel or a commercial building.

Building Salvager
Recover reusable building material from a building that is to be demolished.

Bulldozer Operator
Run heavy equipment to move earth on a construction site.

Bureaucrat
Work at a desk job as a government official.

Bus Dispatcher
Coordinate the movement of buses and ensure that they stay on schedule.

Bus Driver
Drive a bus either within a city or between distant locations.

Bus Mechanic
Repair and maintain a bus.

Business Agent
Handle the business affairs of someone else like an entertainer or represent a union.

Business Manager - artist, performer, athlete
Responsible for the financial and business affairs of their clients.

Busker
A street performer who works for tips.

Butcher
Prepare cuts of meat for sale.

Butler
A servant in a large household.

Buyer
Purchase goods for a company for later resale.

Cabinetmaker
A woodworker who makes kitchen cabinets, furniture and other products. Operates power and hand tools.

Cable Installer
Install and repair cables for cable TV and telecommunication companies.

Cable Splicer
Connect telecommunication cables together overhead, underground and under the sea.

CAD Operator
Use computer design software to draw architectural or engineering plans.

Caddy
Carry golf clubs for someone playing golf and give suggestions on club selection and strategy.

Cafeteria Worker
Prepare and serve food in a large institution like a school or hospital.

Cage Cashier
Work at a casino exchanging cash for chips.

Call Operator
Answer phone calls from customers and clients, answering questions and solving problems.

Calligrapher
Stylish, artistic hand lettering of announcements or certificates.

Camera Operator (TV, movies, videos)
Record and film actors, performers or news for distribution.

Camp Counsellor
Run activities at a summer camp for kids.

Camp Director
In charge of camp counsellors at a summer camp.

Campaign Manager
Direct a political candidate as they run for office, collect funds and direct advertising.

Cannoneer
Fire cannons in the military or for ceremonial purposes.

Captain (boat, plane)
The person in charge of operating a boat or plane.

Caption Writer
Edit TV and movies to provide closed captioning for the hearing impaired.

Car Attendant
Responsible for a sleeping or dining car on a train.

Car Crusher Operator
Work at a junk yard and operate a machine that crushes old cars to be recycled.

Car Designer
An engineer who draws car body designs.

Carnie
An employee at a carnival.

Car Salesperson
Sell new and used cars and trucks at a dealership.

Cardiographer
Operate a machine that records the movements of a patient's heart.

Cardiovascular Technician
Assist physicians in treating heart aliments by operating machines, performing catheterization procedures and preparing patients for tests.

Career Counsellor
Assist people in choosing an occupation.

Caregiver
Tend to someone who has a disability at a residence or institution.

Cargo/Freight Agent
Control the movement of cargo at truck and shipping docks, airlines and train stations.

Carpenter
Work with wood to frame walls, build stairs and complete other construction requirements.

Carpet Cleaner
Use a steam extractor to clean carpets for residential and commercial clients.

Carpet Installer
Lay, cut and fit carpet.

Cartographer
Draw maps.

Cartoonist
Draw cartoons for print, the internet or TV and movies.

Carver
Use knives to shape wood into a desired design.

Cashier
Receive payments and make change at a retail store using a cash register.

Caterer
Make and deliver food for gatherings like weddings and parties.

Cattle Herder
Work at a ranch directing cattle.

Caulker
Apply a sealant around windows, pipes and tubs.

Ceiling Tile Installer
Install ceiling tiles in suspended frames.

Cellist
A musician who plays the cello in an orchestra.

Cellular Technician
Repair cell phones or set up and maintain cellular sites and switching centres.

Cement Mason
Work in construction building foundations, walls and floors.

Censor
Someone working for an organization who edits the content of a performance in TV, movies or radio.

Chairperson
Elected by members of a group to oversee the group's actions and ensure they behave in an orderly fashion.

Chamberlain
A high-ranking official who manages the household of a royal or noble.

Chancellor
The head of an embassy or parliamentary government, a judge or an administrator of a university.

Chaplain
A member of the clergy who gives religious guidance.

Chauffeur
Drive someone in a car to their appointments.

Cheerleader
A member of a squad that encourages a crowd in support of a sports team.

Cheesemaker
Combine milk and a bacterial culture to make cheese.

Chef
Prepare food in a restaurant.

Chemical Engineer
Use chemistry to create new industrial products.

Chemical Plant Worker
Create pharmaceuticals, consumer products and other construction and agricultural products.

Chemist
Work at a university, a government laboratory or in the chemical industry studying the composition and reaction of matter.

Chess Player
Play a strategic board game.

Chicken Sexer
Determine the sex of hatchlings and chickens.

Chief Executive Officer
A CEO is the highest ranking member who has overall control of a company's day-to-day operations.

Chief Financial Officer
A CFO is responsible for financial planning and analysis of financial risk in a corporation.

Chief Mate
The head of a deck department of a merchant ship responsible for the safety and security of the ship.

Child Protective Services Social Worker
Work for a government agency that responds to cases of child abuse or neglect; do investigations and assessments.

Childcare Worker
Work in a daycare or as a pre-school teacher, or provide care for children in some other capacity.

Chimney Sweep
Clean the insides of chimneys of soot and creosote build-up.

Chiropractor
Manipulate the spine or other joints to relive pain and discomfort.

Chocolatier
Make a variety of chocolates.

Choke Setter
Work in the logging industry attaching cable to logs to be pulled out of the woods.

Choreographer (dance)
Determine the movements to be performed during a dance.

Cinematographer
Operate a movie camera to tell a story in an artistic manner.

Circulation Assistant
Work at a magazine or paper maintaining subscriber information.

Circus Freak
Someone with a unique ability who works in a circus.

City Manager
Responsible for all operations of a city.

City Planner
Help to decide the design and layout of the growth of a city.

Civil Engineer
Work to design, build and maintain buildings, roads and bridges.

Civil Servant
An employee of the government.

Claims Adjuster
Investigate insurance claims to determine the amount of liability.

Clarinetist
A musician who plays a clarinet.

Clergyman
A leader within the church like a priest or bishop.

Climate Modeller
A scientist who uses computer simulation to model weather systems.

Climatologist
Study the climate to forecast the weather.

Climber
Ascend mountains, trees or buildings.

Clinical Laboratory Technician
Perform tests to diagnose and treat disease.

Clock Repairer
Fix clocks and watches.

Clockmaker
Make clocks and watches.

Closet Organizer
Help people put their household items away in an organized fashion.

Clown
Dress up in a comical fashion to entertain people at a circus or children's parties.

Coach
Teach a sports team like hockey, football or baseball.

Coal Miner
Work underground digging for coal.

Coastguard
A civilian navel fleet that protects the sovereignty of a country's coastal waters, protects the marine environment and rescues boaters.

Coatroom Attendant
Work at a club taking customers' coats and hanging them up for safe keeping.

Coffin Maker
Design and make caskets for burial.

Colour Printer Operator
Operate developing and photographic printing machines and presses.

Columnist
Write an article daily, weekly or some other set time for a newspaper or magazine.

Comedian
A performer who tells jokes.

Commercial Designer
Create consumer products for a company.

Commercial Diver
Scuba diver who may be involved in construction, salvage, repair work or other underwater activities.

Commodities Trader
Trade stocks for individuals or commercial clients.

Communication Technician
Install and repair the wiring of computer networks and telecommunication equipment.

Community Antenna Television Technician
Maintain the broadband communication systems for TV and data transmission.

Community Support Worker
Work in schools and the community to help children and adults with intellectual and physical disabilities or impairments.

Community Service Manager
Coordinate the activities of a social service program or out-reach program.

Composer
Create music compositions.

Computer Forensic Investigator

Recover data from computers that can be used in the prosecution of criminals.

Computer Information Systems Manager

Plan and direct the computer-related activities of a company or organization.

Computer Operator

Oversee computer hardware systems.

Computer Security Specialist

Ensures that a company's or government's network and data are secure.

Computer Software Engineer/Programmer

Design and code programs that control a computer's actions.

Computer Systems Analyst

Design computer systems to meet the needs of a company or organization.

Concert Poster Artist

Design artwork for concert posters.

Concierge

Help hotel guests with tickets, dining reservations and many other services a guest may require.

Conciliator

Assist parties to resolve a dispute.

Concrete Plant Operator

Work at a plant that makes concrete.

Conductor (music)
Lead a musical orchestra.

Conductor (railroad)
Supervise a passenger or freight train crew.

Confectioner
Make sugar-laden foods like candies and chocolates.

Congressman
A politician who is a member of congress.

Conservation Officer
Enforce laws that protect natural resources, patrol parks and protect wildlife.

Construction Electrician
Install and repair electrical systems.

Construction Formwork Technician
Build forms for concrete stairs, footings and walls.

Construction Worker
Perform various duties on a construction site.

Construction Site Flag Person
Control the flow of traffic around and through a construction site.

Convention Manager
Organize a hotel site for large meetings.

Cook
Prepare food in a restaurant or diner.

Cooking Instructor
Teach methods of preparing food.

Coppersmith
Make articles from copper such as jugs, coffee pots and sculptures.

Copy Editor
Improve the style and readability of written material.

Coroner
Investigate unnatural and unexplained deaths using DNA analysis and autopsies.

Corporate Recruiter
Help companies find employees.

Correctional Officer
Supervise inmates at a prison.

Correspondent
A reporter who reports from the scene of a newsworthy event.

Corrosion Control Technologist
Prevent corrosion of pipes and machinery from environmental effects.

Cosmetologist
A beauty specialist in treating hair, skin and nails.

Cost Estimator
Determine the cost of a construction job.

Costume Attendant
Manage the costumes of a performer.

Costume Designer
Create the clothing a performer will wear in a production.

Counsellor
Advise people on various subjects from mental health issues to course selection for students.

Courier
Deliver parcels.

Court Reporter
Transcribe spoken court proceedings into written form.

Court Usher
Prepare courtrooms, call defendants and supervise jurors.

Cowboy
Perform various duties, usually on a cattle ranch.

Crab Fisherman
Set traps to harvest crabs.

Craft Artist
Make small items for sale at craft fairs.

Craftsman
An artisan who makes decorative or practical items by hand.

Crane Operator
Use a large machine to hoist items around a construction site, rail yard or port.

Creative Director

Oversee the design of advertising, video games or entertainment venues.

Credit Analyst

Evaluate an applicant's loan application and ability to repay it.

Credit Counsellor

Advise clients on managing their debt.

Credit Investigator

Research the credit worthiness of a borrower.

Crime Scene Investigator

Collect evidence at a crime scene to determine what happened.

Crime Scene Cleaner

Clean up stains and fluids from a car, room or other site after a crime and when the investigation is over.

Criminal Investigator

Usually a police officer who attempts to solve crimes and arrest suspects.

Criminologist

Someone who studies crime, criminal actions and social behaviour related to crime.

Crisis Negotiator

Work to resolve tense standoffs without loss of life.

Crocodile Hunter

Hunt crocodiles for inclusion into zoos or removal from residential areas.

Crop Duster

Fly a small plane over a field and apply pesticides.

Crossing Guard

Assist children in crossing the street.

Croupier

A casino employee at a gaming table.

Cruise Ship Worker

Any number of positions on a cruise liner, from crew member to disk jockey, entertainer or aerobics instructor.

Cryptographer

Decipher coded texts, messages or ancient scrolls.

Cultural Attaché

A diplomat who promotes the culture of their homeland.

Curator

The administrative head of a gallery or museum.

Curler

Someone who plays curling.

Custodian

A janitor responsible for the cleanliness of a public building.

Customer Service Representative

Interact with customers to answer questions and to handle complaints.

Customs Agent
Examine goods and baggage at ports of entry into a country to prevent illegal imports and to collect taxes.

Cyberathlete
Compete in computer and video game competitions.

Cyberneticist
Create inanimate objects to behave like living organisms.

Cyclotron Operator
Monitor and maintain a cyclotron for radiopharmaceutical production or atomic research.

Dairy Farmer
Raise cows for milk and milk products.

Dancer
A performer who puts movement to music on stage.

Daredevil
Make jumps on a motorcycle or do spectacular crashes with a car.

Data Entry Operator
Key data into a computer.

Database Administrator
Responsible for the storage and retrieval of data.

Day Spa Attendant
Perform various duties at a spa.

Daycare Worker
Tend to children.

Dealer (Casino)
Work at a gaming table in a casino.

Dean (University)
Head of a faculty at a university.

Deck Officer
Manage a crew on a merchant ship.

Deckhand
Perform various duties on a merchant ship.

Decontamination Technician
Clean up hazardous and toxic spills.

Decorator
Beautify the interior of homes.

Delivery Truck Driver
Transport parcel and freight to their destinations.

Demographer
Do statistical studies of a population.

Demolition Expert
Explode buildings and work at construction and mining sites.

Demolition Worker
Tear down old buildings with machines or explosives.

Dental Assistant
Prepare the dental room, help a dentist during some procedures.

Dental Ceramist
Make porcelain crowns, bridges and dentures.

Dental Hygienist
Clean teeth and gums.

Dentist
Examine teeth, fill cavities and repair damaged teeth.

Deputy
An assistant who can act in their superior's place; for example, a deputy sheriff.

Dermatologist
Skin doctor.

Derrick Operator (Oil and Gas)
Work on oil and gas rigs.

Desktop Publisher
Use a computer and printer to create posters, pamphlets and small books.

Detailer (Automotive)
Clean the interior and exterior of cars and trucks.

Detective
Can work privately or as a member of a police department investigating crimes.

Detention Officer
Oversee inmates at a detention centre.

Diagnostic Medical Sonographer
Use ultrasound to create images of a body.

Diaper Cleaner
Collect diapers and clean them for customers.

Diesel Engine Mechanic
Repair diesel engines.

Dietician
An expert in nutrition. May work at a health club, hospital or for a community organization.

Digital Imaging Technician
Work with a cinematographer to create high quality digital images.

Dinkey Operator
Work at a mine transporting rocks and ore in a shortened train.

Diplomat
A country's representative in a foreign country.

Director - Movies
Control the making of a movie.

Disaster Relief Worker
Go to sites of natural disasters to administer aid.

Disc Jockey
Play music at a night club, over the internet or on the radio.

Dishwasher
Work at a restaurant cleaning dishes.

Dispatcher
Send buses, ambulances, police and fire services to their destinations.

Distiller
Make alcoholic beverages.

Distributor
Send commercial wares to sales outlets.

Dock Crew
Work at a marina or ferry terminal assisting boats to dock.

Dock Labourer
Load and unload vessels.

Doctor
Perform medical procedures.

Documentalist
Assist researchers in finding technical and scientific documents at a library.

Dog Breeder
Mate, raise and sell dogs.

Dog Groomer
Shampoo, trim nails and clean teeth of dogs.

Dog Trainer
Teach dogs how to behave.

Dog Walker
Take other people's dogs for daily walks.

Dogcatcher
Catch stray dogs.

Dolphin Trainer
Train dolphins at an aquarium.

Doorman
Work at a hotel or office opening doors for guests, hailing cabs and guarding the entrance.

Drafter
Prepare technical drawing for buildings, products and other structures.

Drag Queen
A man who dresses in women's clothing, often for performance purposes.

Drag Racer
Race vehicles down a track as fast as possible against an opponent.

Dredge Operator
Operate excavating machines to clear waterways, lakes and streams of bottom sand and gravel.

Dressmaker
Make women's clothing.

Drill Instructor
A non-commissioned officer in the army who teaches recruits.

Drug Enforcement Administration Agent
Police drug dealers and importers.

Drummer
A percussionist in a band.

Dry Cleaner
Clean clothes without water.

Drywall Finisher
Prepare, tape and sand drywall in construction.

Earthquake Geologist
Study and help predict earthquakes.

Ebay Seller
Sell your own goods on an internet auction site.

Ebay Trading Assistant
Sell other people's goods on an internet auction site.

Ebook Publisher
Create a book in an electronic format for distribution.

Ecologist
Study living organisms and their environment.

Economist
Study economics.

Editor
Improve an author's written manuscript.

Educational Official
Work for the government developing educational programs and guidelines.

Egyptologist
Study ancient Egyptian culture.

Elections Officer
Work at a voting site during an election.

Electric Motor Systems Technician
Repair electric motors and transformers.

Electrician
Wire buildings, utility lines, ships and planes.

Electronic Assembler
Work in a factory putting together electronic devices.

Electronic Installer
Install electronic equipment in factories to monitor production or install stereo equipment in automobiles.

Electronics Communications Technician
Install and repair data and telecommunication equipment cabling.

Electronics Technician
Install and repair various electronic equipment.

Electroplater
Use electrolysis to coat articles with a metal film.

Elevator Installer
Install elevators in buildings.

Elevator Mechanic
Repair elevators in buildings.

Embalmer
Work at a funeral home to prepare bodies for burial.

Engraver/Etcher
Cut or acid etch a design onto a hard surface.

Enologist
Study wine and wine making.

Entomologist
One who studies insects.

Entrepreneur
A self-employed business person.

Environmentalist
A person concerned about the environment.

Epidemiologist
Study patterns of disease in a group or culture.

Equipment Manager
Responsible for the equipment of a sports team.

Ergonomist
Design equipment to be more comfortable or make workplace procedures less fatiguing.

Escape Artist
Get out of hand cuffs or locked boxes.

ESL Instructor
Teach English to people whose first language is not English.

Estate Planner
Arrange the financial affairs of a person who is dead or bankrupt.

Evangelist
A Christian who preaches to others and tries to recruit them.

Event Planner
Organize wedding receptions, parties or conventions.

Event Promoter
Publicize an upcoming event.

Examiner
Search municipal records for land titles and restrictions on property.

Excavator
Operate heavy equipment to dig holes on a construction site.

Executioner
Put people to death as punishment for their crimes, by legal sanction.

Explorer
Go to out-of-the-way places to discover things about them.

Explosives Expert
Work at a mine or construction site blowing things up.

Exporter
Send things out of the country for sale.

Exterminator
Kill bugs, rodents, etc. in houses and buildings.

Extra - Movies
Get a small, non-talking part in a movie, often as part of a large crowd.

Fabricator
Read blueprints and construct various consumer items.

Facility Manager
Responsible for the day-to-day running of a company, hotel, or organization.

Falconer
Raise and train birds of prey.

Family Practitioner
A family doctor.

Farmer
Grow crops, raise animals or harvest shellfish.

Farmhand
Assist in the running of a farm.

Farrier
Shoe horses and trim their hooves.

Fashion Designer
Create clothing and accessories.

Fashion Journalist
A reporter who covers the fashion industry and events.

Fast-Food Employee
Cook burgers, operate cash and clean tables.

Federal Bureau of Investigation Agent
A federal officer in the USA.

Fence Builder
Erect fences.

Feng Shui Practitioner
Help organize a living environment to improve qi, or energy flow.

Ferry Worker
Work on a ferry piloting the ship, loading and unloading or maintaining equipment.

Field Engineering Technician
Oversee a construction project to ensure it follows the design specifications.

File Clerk
File records in an office.

Film Critic
Watch movies and write reviews.

Film Editor
Put together a recently shot movie, taking out unwanted frames and joining sections together to create a finished product.

Filmmaker
Direct the making of a movie.

Financial Advisor
Give financial and investment advice.

Financial Aid Officer
Work at a college or university helping students get money to pay for school.

Financial Manager
An accounting professional who oversees the accounting practices of an organization.

Financial Planner
Someone who gives investment advice to people and organizations.

Fire Inspector/Investigator
Conduct safety inspections of local businesses and determine the causes of fires.

Firefighter
Put out residential and industrial fires.

Fish and Game Warden
Ensure fishing and hunting laws are being followed.

Fish Cleaner/Cutter
Work on a vessel or in a processing plant cleaning and trimming fish.

Fish Hatchery Worker
Rear fry in a hatchery.

Fisherman/Woman
Catch fish or other seafood for sale.

Fishing Guide
Take paying customers on fishing trips.

Fishmonger
Sell fish and seafood in a market.

Fitness Worker
Work at a health club instructing clients, maintaining equipment and running the facility.

Flautist
A musician who plays the flute.

Flight Attendant/Steward(ess)
Oversee passengers on board a plane.

Flight Engineer
Part of the flight crew who monitors aircraft systems.

Flight Instructor
Teach people to fly planes or helicopters.

Floor Cleaner
Use machines and mops to clean floors.

Floor Layer
Install flooring.

Floral Designer
Arrange flowers in a way that looks good. Can work in a shop or set up events like weddings.

Florist
Care for and sell flowers.

Folio Artist
Responsible for sound effects in a movie, TV or radio.

Food Critic
Eat at restaurants and write reviews of the food, service and establishment.

Food Preparation Worker
Can work at a fast food restaurant, restaurant or cafeteria preparing food.

Food Scientist
Study the chemistry and sensory nature of food.

Food Service Manager
Oversee food preparation.

Football Player
Play professional football.

Foreign Exchange Trader
Buy and sell foreign currencies.

Foreman
Directly oversee workers on a construction site.

Forensic Accountant
Investigate accounting irregularities for authorities.

Forensic Scientist
Collect crime scene evidence to determine what happened and who may be responsible.

Forest – Faller
Cut down trees.

Forest Fire Fighter
Put out fires in a forest or wooded area.

Forest Fire Inspector
Determine the cause of a forest fire.

Forester
Manage a forest.

Fork Lift Operator
Operate a fork lift to move material.

Forklift Mechanic
Repair fork lifts.

Fortune Teller
Advise people about the future in matters of money, love and luck.

Freight Inspector
Ensure goods for transport are properly loaded, check for illegal goods and check that shipper's paperwork is in order.

Fry Cook
Tend to a deep fryer in a restaurant.

Fundraiser
Help charities raise money.

Funeral Attendant
Assist at a funeral parlour.

Funeral Director/Mortician
Help people with the tasks involved in funeral rites.

Furnace Installer
Install and repair heating units.

Furniture Finisher/Refinisher
Apply final coatings to protect wood furniture and repair damaged furniture.

Furniture Mover
Load furniture into trucks and take it to another destination to unload.

Furrier
Make, repair, clean and store fur coats.

Gadgeteer
Invent and sell things to solve common problems.

Gambler
Play cards or table games for profit.

Game Warden
Protect wildlife.

Gamekeeper
Manage wildlife in a rural area for a land owner.

Game Show Host
Direct contestants competing against one another on a show.

Gaming Surveillance Officer
Work at a casino to prevent cheating.

Garbage Collector
Drive a truck around a route picking up garbage.

Gardener
Grow and maintain plants.

Gas Appliance Repairer
Fix gas appliances like stoves, water heaters and bbqs.

Gas Compressor Operator
Operate valves to control compressors and pumps in a production process.

Gasfitter
Service propane and natural gas systems.

Gastroenterologist
A doctor who specializes in disorders of the throat, stomach, intestines and liver.

Gatekeeper
Someone in an organization who controls the flow of information.

Gem and Diamond Worker/Gem Cutter
Shape and polish diamonds and gems for jewellery or industrial uses.

Gemologist
Expert in gemstones.

Geographer
Study Earth's environment and makeup.

Geologist
Study rocks and minerals.

Geophysicist
Study the Earth's oceans, plate movement and meteorology.

Geoscientist
Study the physical aspects of the Earth.

Geothermal Technician
Service ground-based heating and cooling systems

Geriatric Aide
Assist in the care of the elderly.

Gerontologist
Study the aging process and work with the elderly.

Ghostwriter
A writer who writes a book for someone else.

Gift Basket Provider
Create gift baskets.

Glass Blower
An artist who creates glass works like bowls, drinking glasses and artwork.

Glassmaker
Make glass of all kinds.

Glazier
Install residential and commercial glass.

Goat Herder
Tend to goats.

Goat Soap Maker
Make soap from goat's milk.

Gofer
Perform small tasks such as getting items like coffee or dry cleaning, or running various other errands.

Goldsmith
A metal worker who works with gold.

Golf Course Architect
Design golf courses.

Golf Pro
Work at a golf course pro shop giving lessons.

Golfer
Play golf for money.

Gondolier
Ferry tourists in boats using a pole.

Gossip Columnist
Write about celebrities.

Grader Operator
Operate heavy equipment on a construction site to level roads, etc.

Graphic Artist/Designer
Create a visual identity for clients for ads, business cards and web sites.

Gravedigger
Dig holes for burial.

Greenskeeper
Tend to the lawn at a gold course or sports field.

Greeter
Meet customers as they enter a store.

Grief Counsellor .
Help people deal with the death of a loved one or other trauma.

Grip
Work on a movie set moving and securing scenery, lights and cameras.

Grocer
Sell items in a grocery store.

Grocery Bagger
Work at a checkout line putting groceries into bags.

Groomer - Animals
Tend to animals to improve their appearance and health.

Grounds Keeper
Maintain a baseball or football field.

Grounds Maintenance Worker
Maintain golf course and sports field equipment.

Guidance Councillor
Advise students at schools.

Guitar Maker
Make and repair guitars.

Guitarist
A musician who plays the guitar.

Gunsmith
Build and repair firearms.

Guru
A person with great spiritual knowledge who offers guidance to others.

Gym Attendant
Supervise people using a gym facility and maintain its cleanliness.

Gymnast
Perform complex athletic exercise routines.

Gynecologist
A doctor specializing in women's health.

Haberdasher
Sell men's clothing and accessories.

Hairdresser/Hairstylist
Cut, style and tend to women's hair.

Handwriting Analyst
Work in law enforcement studying handwriting traits and characteristics.

Handyman
Do minor home repairs and maintenance tasks.

Harbour Pilot
Assist in docking ships and guiding them through busy waterways.

Hardwood Floor Installer
Lay down hardwood flooring.

Harpist
A musician who plays the harp.

Hazardous Material Worker
Clean up spills of dangerous chemicals.

Headmaster/Headmistress
Run a private school.

Health Care Administrator
Direct health care in a department or an entire facility.

Health Educator
Teach about health-related topics.

Health Information Technician
Maintain patient records at a hospital or clinic.

Health Inspector
Ensure restaurants are running a clean and safe operation.

Health Records Administrator
Maintain the health records of patients.

Health Service Manager
Oversee healthcare for a department or an entire organization.

Heating, Air-conditioning and Refrigeration Technician
Install and maintain the environmental control systems of a building.

Heavy Duty Equipment Technician/Mechanic
Repair heavy equipment.

Heavy Equipment Operator
Operate large machinery at a construction site.

Helicopter Pilot
Fly a helicopter.

Herbalist
Someone with knowledge in herbal medicine and treatments.

Highway Patrol
A policy officer responsible for vehicle traffic.

Historian
Record, catalogue and maintain records of historical events.

Hockey Player
Play professional hockey.

Hoist/Winch Operator
Control powered machines that use cables to lift loads.

Home Appliance Repair
Repair household appliances on site or at a repair shop.

Home Entertainment System Installer
Set up TV and stereo equipment.

Home Health Aide
Assist physically impaired people in their homes.

Home Inspector
Evaluate and record any problems with residential or commercial property.

Homemaker
Responsible for household duties.

Horse Breeder
Select and breed horses to enhance specific characteristics.

Horse Groomer
Tend to the physical care of horses.

Horse Trainer
Teach horses to perform and behave in particular ways.

Horseback Riding Instructor
Teach people how to ride a horse.

Horticulture Technician
Tend to plants, bushes and trees outside and in greenhouses.

Hospice Nurse
Tend to terminally ill patients.

Hospital Administrator
Manage the business aspects of a hospital.

Hospitality Worker
Work as a cook or server, or bus tables.

Hosteller
Someone who keeps a hostel for travellers to stay at.

Hot Air Balloonist
Fly a hot air balloon.

Hot Tar Roofer
Use hot tar to install and repair flat roofs.

Hotel Desk Clerk
Greet guests, check them in and assist with their stays.

Hotel Manager
Run a hotel.

House Painter
Paint the interior and exterior of houses.

House Sitter
A person who stays at someone else's house when they are away for an extended period of time.

Housecleaner/Housekeeper
A person who cleans someone's house.

Human Billboard
People who place advertisements on their bodies for a period of time.

Human Resources Assistants
Help maintain employee records.

Human Resources Manager/Specialist
Responsible for employee documents and policies.

Hunter/Trapper
Hunt and trap animals for their hides.

Hydraulic Crane Operator
Operate a crane to lift loads.

Hydraulic Service Mechanic
Repair hoists and other lifting units.

Hydrologist
Study the flow and control of water.

Hypnotist
An entertainer or wellness practitioner who influences behaviours by suggestion.

Illusionist
A magician.

Illustrator
Draw pictures or diagrams.

Image Consultant
Help others look and act their best.

Impersonator
Dress up and act like someone else.

Importer
Bring merchandise into a country for resale.

Impressionist
Copy the voices and mannerisms of famous people.

Inboard/Outboard Mechanic
Repair boat motors.

Income Tax Preparer
Fill out tax forms for people.

Industrial Designer
Study and improve the form and function of consumer products.

Industrial Engines and Equipment Parts Person
Order and track parts for the repair of heavy machinery.

Industrial Instrument Mechanic
Maintain sensors, medical equipment, fire and burglar alarms.

Industrial Mechanic (Millwright)
Repair industrial machinery.

Industrial Warehouseperson
Store and distribute parts and materials used in construction and in plants.

Infantryman
Soldier in the army.

Infomericial Spokesperson
Sell consumer products in advertisements 30-60 minutes long.

Infopreneur
Create and sell an information product.

Information Officer
Distribute information for an organization internally, or liaison with the press.

Innkeeper
Maintain a place for travellers to stay.

Insulation Installer/Technician
Install residential and commercial insulation material.

Insurance Agent
Sell automobile, life and home insurance.

Intelligence Officer
Analyze information for a government organization or private company.

Interior Designer
Create functional and aesthetic living environments.

Internal Auditor
Check a company's accounting or computer procedures for reliability.

Interpreter
Convert one language to another either verbally or in writing.

Interviewer
A reporter who asks people questions.

Inventor
Convert ideas to objects to solve a problem or create new devices.

Investigator
A member of the police force or a private company who analyzes a crime or a person's background.

Investment Banker
A banker who trades securities and is involved with corporate mergers and acquisitions.

Ironworker
Put up the steel structure of a building.

Janitor
Keep businesses and institutions clean.

Jester
A fool who entertains and tells jokes while wearing bright clothing and a three-point hat.

Jeweller
Make and sell jewellery.

Jockey
Ride horses in a race.

Journalist
Report on newsworthy current events.

Judge
Oversee legal proceedings.

Judicial Worker
Assist in the operation of a court.

Juggler
An entertainer who throws various items into the air in rapid succession and catches them.

Kelp Harvester
Collect kelp from the sea for human consumption and animal feed.

Kennel Worker
Assist in the care of dogs.

Kinesiologist
Knowledgeable in anatomy and the mechanics of body movement.

Knitting Machine Operator
Operate machines that process yarn into woven clothing.

Labour Relations Manager
Facilitate negotiations between employers and workers.

LAN Administrator
Oversee a computer network.

Landscape Architect
Design outdoor public spaces that are in harmony with their surrounding environments.

Landscape Horticulturist
Use plants and trees in designing an outdoor space.

Lathe Operator
Turn wood or metal on a spinning machine to create a work of art or a mechanical piece.

Lather
Build interior walls with narrow strips of wood and plaster.

Law Clerk
A novice lawyer who works as an assistant to a lawyer or judge.

Lawn and Garden Maintenance Person
Tend to gardens and cut and edge lawns.

Lawyer
A legal advisor.

Leasing Manager
Advise customers about leasing choices.

Leather Worker
Make clothing items out of leather.

Leech Trapper
Catch leeches for sale as fish bait.

Legal Assistant
Help lawyers prepare legal documents and conduct research.

Lego Builder
Contracted to build large objects out of Lego building blocks.

Lens Grinder
Make optical products like camera lenses and glasses.

Lexicographer
Write and edit a dictionary.

Librarian
Manage the books in a library.

Life Coach
Advise people on choices they make concerning their lives.

Lifeguard
Oversee swimmers.

Lighthouse Keeper
Maintain a lighthouse.

Line Installer/Repairer
Run cables for electricity, voice and data communications.

Line Splicer
Connect communication cables together.

Linesman
A football official or an assistant to an umpire or referee in tennis or soccer.

Linguist
Expert at many languages.

Lion Tamer
Teach lions to perform before a crowd.

Liquid Waste Treatment Plant Operator
Process sewage at a treatment plant.

Literary Critic
Write a review of books you have read.

Litho Pressperson (Web, Sheet Fed, Rotary & Gravure)
Operate a printing press.

Loan Officer
Determine whether a customer qualifies to borrow money from a financial institution.

Lobbyist
A representative of a political party, business or interest group who tries to influence political decisions.

Locksmith
Install locks and make keys.

Locomotive Engineer
Drive a train.

Log Builder
Put up buildings constructed of logs and timbers.

Logger
Cut down trees for the forestry industry.

Logistics and Distribution Manager
Oversee the distribution and control of inventory.

Loss Prevention Officer
Detect and prevent retail theft by customers and employees.

Lubrication Technician
Keep automobiles or machinery running.

Lumberjack
Cut down trees using hand tools.

Lyricist
Write words for songs.

Machinist
Repair machines or operate a machine like a lathe in a factory.

Maggot Farmer
Raise maggots for fish bait.

Magician
An entertainer who does tricks of illusion.

Magistrate
A judge in a lower court.

Maid/Housekeeper
Clean and keep up someone's house.

Mail Carrier/Clerk/Handler
Work at the post office sorting or delivering mail.

Maitre d'
Head waiter who takes reservations, assigns tables and oversees the serving staff.

Makeup Artist
Apply makeup to actors or models in movies, TV or fashion shows.

Mall Cart Business Operator
Sell goods like jewellery or sunglasses from a cart in a mall.

Manicurist
Beautify fingers and hands in a nail salon.

Manservant
Be a person's personal servant.

Marine Biologist
Study plants and animals of the sea.

Marine Cargo Inspector
Inspect cargo and assorted paperwork of goods being shipped abroad or coming into port.

Marine Engineer
Maintain various systems on board a vessel.

Marine Mechanical/Repair Technician
Repair inboard and outboard engines and other systems of watercraft.

Market Researcher/Surveyor
Poll people to get their opinions on products or advertising.

Marketing
Develop branding and advertising to promote goods and services for sale.

Marketing Manager
Direct a marketing program and staff.

Marksman
An expert shot with a weapon like a rifle.

Marriage Therapist
Help couples resolve their differences.

Massage Therapist/Masseuse
Perform body conditioning for therapeutic and medical purposes.

Matador
Fight bulls in a ring.

Mathematician
Teach or use mathematics to solve problems.

Mayor
Top municipal employee who runs a city or town.

Meat Packer
Work at a meat processing plant packaging products for shipping to a retail butcher or store.

Meat Cutter
Prepare cuts of meat.

Media Consultant
Provide positive press coverage for a client.

Mediator
Help resolve conflicts between two or more people or groups.

Medical Assistant
Keep track of records, do laboratory work and perform administrative tasks in a medical office.

Medical Laboratory Technologist
Run tests on fluids and tissue samples to detect disease.

Medical Sonographer
Operate ultrasound machines for diagnostic purposes.

Mercenary
Private soldier for hire.

Merchandiser
Maintain the display of a product line in a retail store for a manufacturer or distributor.

Messenger
Deliver packages by truck, car or bicycle.

Metal Fabricator/Fitter
Make or repair items made out of metal at a factory or construction site.

Metallurgist
Study the properties of metals.

Meteorologist
Study the atmosphere and predict weather.

Metre Reader
Walk around taking readings from gas or electric metres.

Metre Technician
Install and repair electronic metres in homes and businesses.

Microbiologist
Study bacteria and other microbes.

Midwife
Provide care to expectant mothers. Can deliver babies at home.

Midshipman
A low ranking officer in the navy.

Milker
Obtain the milk from cows, goats, etc.

Millwright
Build and repair machines at a factory.

Mime
An entertainer who acts out a story without speaking. Often wears white facial makeup and silly clothing.

Miner
Work underground removing ore.

Mineralogist
Know minerals and how to find them.

Mini-Putt Professional
Play miniature golf for money.

Missionary
A religious group member sent to promote their beliefs in other countries.

Mobile Crane Operator
Operate a hoisting crane on construction sites to lift items to their location.

Model
Work in the fashion industry to show off clothing, makeup and accessories.

Model Maker
Make miniature displays for architects, manufacturers or inventors.

Mold Maker
Create molds to cast metal or plastic items.

Monk
A male member of a religious group who withdraws from society to live in a religious community devoted to prayer and solitude.

Mosquito Control Officer
Spray for mosquitoes and assist homeowners in identifying mosquito breeding sites.

Motivational Speaker
Give inspirational talks to groups.

Motocross Rider
Ride a motorcycle.

Motorcycle Mechanic
Repair motorcycles.

Motorcycle Racer
Race motorcycles cross country or at a drag strip.

Mountain Biker
Ride a mountain bike for pay.

Mountain Rescuer
Work at a resort area helping people injured in mountainous areas.

Mountaineer
Climb mountains.

Mountain Man
Live by yourself off the land having a completely self-contained lifestyle.

Mover
Transport furniture from one location to another by truck.

Movie Critic
Write reviews about movies you have seen.

Muralist
Draw pictures on walls.

Museum Technician
Work at a museum, tending to exhibits.

Music Critic
Write a review of music or a band you have listened to.

Music Promoter
Advertise upcoming bands at a venue.

Musician
Play a musical instrument for a living.

Mystery Shopper
Buy items at retail stores and report on your shopping experience.

Nanny
Tend to other people's children in their home.

Narrator
Tell a story of an event in radio or TV.

Naturopath
Experienced in natural health remedies.

Navigator
Map out and ensure a ship or a plane gets to its destination.

Navy
Work in the navy on sea-going vessels.

Negotiator
Help solve differences between two or more people or groups.

Net Maker
Make and repair nets on a trawler.

Neuroscientist
Doctor of the brain and nervous system.

News Reporter
Gather facts about newsworthy events.

Notary Public
Someone who can certify authenticity of documents and signatures.

Novelist
Write fiction books.

Nuclear Engineer
Study sub-atomic physics.

Nuclear Medicine Technician
Use radioactive isotopes in treating and diagnosing disease.

Nuclear Plant Worker
Work at a nuclear power plant.

Numerologist
Use numbers to predict the future.

Nun
A female member of a religious order who devotes herself to religious study.

Nurse
Care for patients at a hospital.

Nursemaid
Look after young children.

Nutritionist
An expert in nutrition.

Obstetrician
A baby or pregnancy doctor.

Occupational Therapist
A therapist who involves a patient in a work activity as part of their treatment.

Oceanographer
Study the ocean.

Office Clerk
Maintain records in an office.

Office Manager
Direct the daily activities in an office.

Oil Burner Mechanic
Install and repair household and industrial oil-fired appliances.

Oil Change Technician
Change oil and perform routine maintenance tasks at a garage.

Oilfield Worker
Work in the oil fields on a rig.

Oil Tank Removal Technician
Remove old oil tanks from homes and businesses.

Ombudsman
Investigate complaints against the government.

Oncologist
A doctor specializing in cancer.

Online Business Operator
Run a business over the internet.

Opaquer
Colour in animation cells.

Opera Singer
Sing in operas.

Ophthalmic Laboratory Technician
Make prescription eye wear.

Optician
Fit and sell eye wear.

Optometrist
Examine eyes and prescribe vision corrective devices.

Oracle
Someone with a vast amount of knowledge and wisdom.

Order Filler
Prepare items for shipping that a remote customer has purchased.

Organist
A musician who plays the organ.

Organization Development Consultant
Provide business advice to small companies and organizations.

Organizer
Helps people put things like clothing away in an orderly fashion.

Ortho Technician
Apply and remove casts and splints for injured limbs.

Outdoor Power Equipment Technician
Repair all-terrain vehicles, jet skis, snowmobiles or any other outdoor equipment.

Packer
Prepare items for moving.

Painter
Paint residential and commercial properties.

Painter (Arts)
An artist who paints landscapes, portraits, etc.

Paleontologist
Study prehistoric life, including dinosaurs.

Palm Reader
A fortune teller who reads palms.

Paparazzi
Photographers who hound celebrities and take their picture.

Paper Carrier
Deliver newspapers door to door.

Paralegal
Someone who assists a lawyer.

Paramedic
A member of an ambulance crew who performs emergency medical care.

Park Ranger
Protect and preserve parkland.

Parker
Work at a parking lot parking vehicles.

Parking Enforcement Officer
Write parking tickets.

Parking Lot Attendant
Control access to a parking lot and collect fees.

Parks Planner
Design the appearance of a park.

Parole Officer
Maintain contact with people recently released from prison.

Parts and Warehousing Person
Keep track of inventory in a warehouse.

Pastor
A Christian minister.

Patent Attorney
A lawyer knowledgeable in protecting inventors' ideas.

Pathologist
Medical professional dealing with tissue or laboratory test diagnosis.

Paver
Use heavy machinery to lay asphalt, or put down paving stones to make walkways.

Pawnbroker
Lend money in exchange for an item of value.

Payroll Administrator
In charge of paying employees at a company.

Payroll Clerk
Work in a payroll department.

Pediatrician
A doctor specializing in treating children.

Percussionist
A musician who makes music hitting an object and making it vibrate like drums, cymbals or bells.

Perfumer
Make and sell perfume.

Perfusionist
Operate a heart-lung machine during surgery.

Perioperative Nurse
Care for patients before, during and after surgery.

Personal Assistant
Someone who helps a businessperson or celebrity with a variety of tasks.

Personal Groomer
Work for a celebrity to ensure they look their best.

Personal Shopper
Buy required or wanted items for a businessperson or celebrity.

Personal Trainer
Teach someone one-on-one about physical fitness.

Pest Control Technician
Kill pests and bugs in homes and commercial buildings.

Pet Psychiatrist
Provide emotional care for pets.

Pet Psychic
Communicate with dead pets.

Pet Sitter
Take care of someone's pet while they are at work or away for an extended period of time.

Petroleum Engineer
Work in the exploration and development of oil and gas.

Pewter Worker
Make tableware or artistic pieces with metal that is mostly tin.

Pharmaceutical Sales Representative
Sell drugs to stores and give sample to doctors.

Pharmacist
Dispense medications in a retail environment.

Pharmacologist
A doctor who researches the effects of drugs and chemicals.

Pharmacy Aide/Technician
Help a pharmacist.

Philanthropist
Improve humanity through charitable activities.

Philosopher
A thinker who attempts to explain reality and human events.

Phlebotomist
Someone who draws blood for testing or donations.

Phone Installer
Put telephone wiring in a home or office.

Photoengraver
Reproduce illustrations using photographic techniques on a metal plate.

Photogrammetrist
Use photographic images to create maps and in geological surveying.

Photographer
Take pictures using a camera.

Photographic Processing Worker
Develop photographic film.

Physical Therapist
Help patients with muscular pain or injuries regain use and mobility of a limb.

Physician
A doctor.

Physicist
Study sub-atomic particles and the behaviour of the universe.

Pianist
A musician who plays the piano.

Piano Tuner
Improve the tone and sound of a piano.

Pilates Instructor
Teach the physical exercises of Pilates.

Pile Driver
Pound piles into the ground for supports for building, docks and bridges.

Pipefitter
Install and repair mechanical piping systems.

Planermill Maintenance Technician
Repair planers and planermill equipment.

Plasterer
Apply plaster on walls or decorative molding.

Plastic Surgeon
A cosmetic surgeon.

Playwright
Write plays.

Plumber
Install and repair pipes and fixtures.

Podiatrist
A foot doctor.

Poet
Write imaginative verses.

Police Officer
Enforce the laws of society.

Policy Advisor
A political aide who gives advice on proposed legislation or programs.

Political Aide
Help a politician perform their duties.

Political Campaign Worker
Promote your political candidate by erecting signs and making phone calls.

Political Scientist
Study the political system.

Politician
Someone who runs for a governmental office.

Polling Agent
Oversee the election at a polling station and verify the identities of voters.

Polymer Scientist
A chemist with knowledge of large, repeating molecules held together by chemical bonds.

Pond and Water Gardener
Install and maintain ponds and associated plants and aquatic animals.

Pope
Head of the Roman Catholic Church.

Portable Toilet Cleaner
Clean out portable toilets.

Porter
Carry luggage at an airport or railway station.

Postal Worker
Sort and deliver mail.

Power Line Technician
Repair overhead and underground electrical systems.

Power Plant Operator
Work at a nuclear or hydroelectric facility that makes electricity.

Presenter
Introduce people to an audience or give out awards at a ceremony.

President
The head of state of a country.

Priest
An ordained Christian minister.

Prime Minister
The head of cabinet in a parliamentary system.

Principal
The head administrator of a school.

Printer
Make books, magazines or advertising material.

Prison Guard
Oversee prisoners.

Private Investigator
A detective hired by private individuals or companies to collect evidence on some civil matter.

Probation Officer
Supervise recently released prisoners.

Process Engineer
Specialize in manufacturing articles from raw materials, designing equipment and creating consumer and industrial products.

Proctologist
Specialist treating issues in the colon, rectum and anus.

Producer (Movies)
Involved in all phases of the film-making process.

Product Demonstrator
Work in retail environments showing prospective customers how to use a product.

Product Tester
Try products to ensure that they work as they are suppose to.

Professor
College teacher.

Program Coordinator
Direct activities at an amusement park or college.

Project Manager
Direct the resources needed to complete a task.

Projectionist
Operate the movie projector in a cinema.

Promoter
Advertise and let the public know about an upcoming event.

Proofreader
Detect and correct errors in written work.

Property Manager
Oversee property like an apartment complex or a commercial property.

Psychiatrist
Treat mental disorders.

Psychic
Predict future events.

Psychologist
Provide therapy for mental disorders.

Public Relations Specialist
Someone who acts as a representative of a company in dealings with the media.

Public Speaker
Someone who give speeches before a crowd.

Publicist
A promoter who gets favourable press for a client.

Publisher (Books)
Produce and distribute information.

Purchasing Agent/Clerk
Buy goods for a company or governmental department.

Pundit
A critic who expresses an opinion.

Puppeteer
Move an inanimate object to simulate a living person or animal.

Quality Control Technician
Ensure manufacturing standards at a plant are being met.

Quartermaster
An army or naval officer.

Rabbi
A Jewish religious leader.

Race Car Driver
Drive cars in races.

Race Queen
A promotional model at a car racing event.

Radio Announcer
Talk on the radio.

Radiation/Radiology Therapist
Treat cancer using x-rays, gamma rays and electrons.

Radio Operator
Uses radio equipment to communicate in the military.

Railroad Worker
Work in a rail yard.

Railway Car Technician
Repair rail cars.

Rancher
Own and manage a ranch.

Rapper
Artist who delivers rhythmic spoken songs.

Rare Book Dealer
Buy and sell hard-to-finds books.

Rat Catcher
Catch rodents.

Real Estate Appraiser
Estimate the value of property for a customer.

Real Estate Assessor
Estimate the value of real estate for the government for tax purposes.

Real Estate Broker
Sell properties.

Real Estate Conveyancer
Transfer property title between two parties.

Real Estate Developer
Build properties.

Receptionist
Work in an office answering phones and greeting customers.

Recording Engineer
Work in a studio mixing, editing and recording music or other sounds.

Recreation Attendant
Work at an amusement park, skating rink or other facility doing various jobs.

Recreation Coordinator
Manager of a recreation facility.

Recreation Vehicle Service Technician
Repair recreation vehicles.

Recruiter
Hire people to work for a company, sports team or the armed forces.

Referee
Enforce rules in a sport like hockey, soccer or boxing.

Reflexologist
An alternative medical method of massaging pressure points of the hands, feet or ears to relieve symptoms.

Refrigeration & Air Conditioning Mechanic
Install and repair cooling systems in homes and buildings.

Registered Nurse
Care for patients in a medical facility like a hospital.

Rehabilitation Assistants
Work under a physical therapist to help patients recover from injuries.

Reinforcing Steel Installer
Place rebar in formwork on a construction site.

Researcher
Gather facts to produce reports that assist others in the decision-making process.

Reservation Agent
Book cars or air travel seats for customers.

Resident Care Aid/Attendant
Assist a nurse in a retirement home.

Residential Building Maintenance Worker
Perform various repair duties in homes.

Residential Construction Framing Technician
Build frames for houses.

Residential Steep Roofer
Install and repair roofs that are on a steep angle.

Respiratory Therapist
Treat and care for patients who have breathing difficulties.

Restaurateur
Own and operate a restaurant.

Restoration Expert
Repair photographs and paintings.

Resumé Writer
Write resumés for people seeking employment.

Retail Sales Person
Perform various duties at a retail store.

Returning Officer
Oversee elections in one or more constituencies of a parliamentary system.

Revenue Agent
Work for the tax department.

Rig Technician
Work on oil and gas drilling rigs.

Rigger
Install and maintain the sails, masts and cordage of sailing ships.

Ringmaster
The leader of a circus.

Road Builder and Heavy Construction
An entry-level position in road construction.

Robotics Engineer
Build robots mainly for industrial assembly.

Rock Quarry Worker
Work in a quarry processing rock for the construction industry.

Rock Splitter
Use machines to split and cut rocks and bricks at a quarry or for construction.

Rock Star
An entertainer in a rock and roll band.

Rock Wall Builder
Use rocks and bricks to construct walls.

Rocket Scientist
Work in a space program or the military designing rockets and spacecraft.

Roof and Gutter Cleaner
Use pressure washers to clean roofs and gutters on homes.

Roofer
Install various roofing materials.

Rope Maker
Construct rope using machines or by hand.

Roughneck
A semi-skilled worker on an oil rig.

Roustabout
General labourer on an oil rig or circus.

Sail Maker
Make sails for boats.

Sailor
Perform various duties on a sailing vessel.

Sales Clerk
Work at a retail store.

Sales Manager
Direct salespeople or be in charge of sales in a territory.

Sales Representative
Sell products for a manufacturer or wholesaler.

Salesperson
Work at a retail store.

Salt Miner
Extract salt from the ground.

Saxophonist
A musician who plays the saxophone.

Scanner Operator
Control electronic scanners used in lithographic printing.

School Administrator
Direct staffing and day-to-day operations in a school.

School Bus Driver
Drive a bus on a route delivering children to school.

School Principal
The head of a school.

Scout
Watch junior sports for up-and-coming talented players to sign to a professional team. Also applies to other talents such as modelling, acting, music, etc.

Scrabble Player
Play Scrabble for money.

Scraper Operator
Operate heavy equipment to level ground on a construction site.

Screenwriter
Write scripts for movies and TV.

Sculptor
Create art out of stone or clay.

Seaman
Perform various duties on a sea-going vessel.

Seamstress
Sew clothing.

Search Engine Optimization Specialist
Help web sites rank higher in search engine results.

Second Mate
The third in charge on a merchant ship.

Secret Agent
A spy engaged in gathering secret information from another government. Work for the CIA or CSIS.

Secret Service Agent
An investigator with a federal crime bureau like the FBI or CSIS.

Secretary
Perform administrative tasks in an office.

Secretary Treasurer
Responsible for financial policies for an organization or government.

Security Analyst
Determine the threats and safeguard information, buildings or countries.

Securities Analyst
Study stock market offerings.

Security Alarm Installer
Put alarm systems into homes and buildings.

Security Guard
Patrol an area to safeguard it from thieves or vandals.

Seismologist
Study earthquakes.

Septic Tank Installer/Cleaner
Put in and clean residential onsite wastewater systems.

Servant
A domestic worker in a large household.

Service Station Attendant
Pump gas at a service station.

Set Designer
Create scenery for stage, TV or movies.

Set Dresser
Help actors change into the correct costumes.

Sewage Treatment Plant Operator
Work at a waste treatment plant.

Sewer Inspector
Go into sewers to inspect pipes.

Sexologist
An expert in human sexuality.

Shampooer
Wash and style hair at a salon.

Sharpshooter
An expert firearms marksman.

Sheep Castrator
Remove sheep testicles.

Sheep Shearer
Shave the wool off of sheep.

Sheet Metal Worker
Work with metal to form heating and cooling ducts, gutters or anything else made with sheet metal.

Shepherd
Tend a flock of sheep.

Sheriff
A legal officer in a county.

Ship Carpenter and Jointer
Install and repair woodwork in boats.

Ship Loader
Load and unload vessels.

Shipping and Receiving Clerk
Send out and receive goods and maintain the appropriate records.

Shipwright
Build ships.

Shoe Shiner
Polish shoes.

Shoemaker
Make shoes.

Shopper
Purchase goods for other people.

Shrimper
Fish for shrimp.

Shuttle Car/Bus Operator
Transport people a short distance between two points like an airport to a hotel.

Sign Language Interpreter
Communicate with a hearing impaired person using hand gestures.

Signalman
A communications person on a vessel or in a rail yard.

Silversmith
Create jewellery, sculpture and silverware using silver and other metals.

Singer
Use the voice to sing songs.

Singles Event Coordinator
Bring together single people for an event like dinner, games or speed dating.

Site Supervisor
In charge of a construction site.

Skateboarder
Ride a skateboard professionally.

Sketch Artist
Quickly draw portraits at fairs or work for the police department to draw suspects.

Ski/Snowboard Instructor
Teach skiing or snowboarding.

Ski Hill Groomer
Maintain ski runs at a resort.

Ski Patrol
Assist injured or lost skiers.

Skidder
Drive a vehicle that pulls logs out of the forest.

Skier
Ski for money.

Skinner
Install siding.

Sky Marshal
An undercover police officer on a plane.

Slaughterhouse Worker
Work at a meat packing and processing plant.

Slime Eel Fisher
Catch slime eels for food in Korea.

Small Business Owner
Own and operate your own business.

Small Engine Mechanic
Repair lawn mowers, chainsaws and outboard motors.

Snake Charmer
An entertainer who works with snakes.

Snake Wrangler
Catch and remove snakes from homes and businesses.

Snake/Spider Venom Extractor
Milk snakes and spiders for their venom for medical study.

Snow Plow Operator
Clear roadways, parking lots and driveways of snow.

Snowmobile Mechanic
Repair snowmobiles.

Soccer Player
Play professional soccer.

Social Scientist
Study human society.

Social Worker
Assist people with their lives and help solve family problems.

Soil Scientist
Categorize soil by type and use and determine soil fertility and nutrient analysis.

Soldier
Fight in the armed forces.

Solicitor
A lawyer.

Sommelier
A wine expert. Can work in restaurants recommending wine and food pairings.

Songwriter
Write songs.

Sound Engineer
Edit, mix and record music or other recordings.

Spa Therapist
Perform massages, hot stone therapy or acupressure at a spa.

Special Effects Expert
Work in the movie industry using computers and various other technologies to create movie magic.

Speech Pathologist/Therapist
Study and treat speech disorders.

Speech Writer
Write speeches for politicians or business people.

Spelunker
A person who explores caves.

Spin Doctor
Work for a political organization or business directing the press as to your client's point of view.

Sports Announcer
Speak on TV or radio describing a sporting event for the listeners and viewers.

Sprinkler System Installer
Install fire suppression systems.

Spy
Work for a government or company to gather information on a rival.

Squeegee Person
Clean windshields on street corners for spare change.

Stage Technician
Perform a variety of jobs in the theatre from setting up props to handling light and sound requirements.

Stable Worker
Work at a farm for horses.

Statistician
Use mathematics to explain or predict human behaviour for governments or private organizations.

Steamfitter/Pipefitter
Install and repair pipes that can carry water, chemicals or steam.

Steeplejack
Inspect and maintain high structures like cell towers, church spires and bridges.

Stenographer
Transcribe dictation in an office or the testimony in a court.

Sterile Supply Technician
Decontaminate and sterilize medical equipment and dressings.

Stevedore
A dock worker who loads and unloads vessels.

Steward - Airline, Passenger Ships
Assist passengers on a plane or cruise ship.

Stock Broker
Buy and sell shares and other securities.

Stock Trader
A person who buys and sells shares and other securities.

Stone Sawyer/Stonecutter
Cut rough blocks of stone at a quarry for further processing.

Stonemason
Build walls and chimneys using bricks.

Store Detective
Detect and deter retail theft.

Store Manager
Run the daily operations of a retail store.

Storm Drain Cleaner
Remove sand, garbage and debris from storm drains.

Storyteller
An entertainer who relays the contents of a story in a captivating manner.

Strategic Communications Professional
Promote the message of a government or corporation for long-term benefit.

Street Artist
Use chalk or paint to put images on sidewalks or walls in public places.

Street Musician
Play a musical instrument in public for money.

Street Performer
Entertain people in a public place by singing, dancing, juggling, etc.

Street Sweeper
Drive a sweeper to clean streets.

Street Vendor
Sell items to the public from a street location.

Streetcar Operator
Drive a streetcar to transport people.

Strength Trainer
Coach people in exercises to increase their strength.

Strongman
Compete in feats of strength.

Structural Engineer
Design structures that support or resist a load like a building or a bridge.

Student Life Programmer
Direct events at a college.

Stuffer
Place advertising in envelopes.

Stunt Person
Perform physical stunts for an actor.

Stylist
Cut and style hair.

Substance Abuse Counsellor
Advise people on how to deal with and overcome addictions.

Subway Operator
Drive a subway car.

Superintendent of Schools
Oversee a group of schools in a district.

Surgeon
A doctor who performs operations.

Surveyor
Determine the exact position of property and land boundaries.

Swimming Instructor
Teach people to swim.

Swimming Pool Cleaner
Clean swimming pools.

Swineherd
Looks after pigs.

Sword Swallower
A performer who puts swords down their throat.

Swordsmith
Make swords.

Syndicated Columnist
Write a daily, weekly or monthly article for a paper or magazine.

System Administrator
Oversee a computer system or network.

Systems Analyst
Recommend software and hardware solutions for a business or organization.

Systems Designer
Integrate computer equipment into a system to satisfy a computing requirement.

Table Tennis Player
Play professions table tennis.

Tailor
Sell and repair clothing.

Talent Manager
Search for talented entertainers to represent.

Talent Scout
Work for a sporting team, modelling agency, music label or movie studio searching for up-and-coming talent.

Tanner
Process hides into leather.

Tarot Card Reader
Predict someone's future using tarot cards.

Tattooist
Put tattoos on people.

Tax Collector
Work for the government collecting unpaid taxes.

Tax Examiner
Examine and review tax returns for accuracy.

Tax Preparer
Fill out tax returns for other people.

Taxi Driver
Transport people by car or van.

Taxidermist
Stuff and mount dead animals for display.

Taxi Dispatcher
Takes customers' calls and send available taxis to pick them up.

Teacher
Work at a school educating students.

Teaching Assistant
Help a teacher; usually in college.

Technical Support Specialist
Answer phone calls and help solve computer-related problems.

Telecontrol Technologist
Install and maintain telecommunication cables and phone equipment.

Telemarketer
Call people up at dinner time and try to sell them something they don't want.

Telephone Operator
Help customers make their telephone connections.

Teller
Work at a bank assisting customers with their banking.

Tenant Support Worker
A mental health care worker who helps people with their housing requirements.

Tennis Instructor
Teach people how to play tennis.

Terrazzo Worker
Set marble chips into cement floors and panels to create designs that simulate marble.

Test Pilot
Fly experimental aircraft.

Textile Worker
Work in a mill making clothing.

Theologian
Study God.

Think Tank Person
Use creativity to come up with possible solutions to various problems.

Ticket Taker
Stand at an entrance to a venue collecting tickets from paid customers and giving back a ticket stub.

Ticket Agent
Sell tickets to an event.

Ticket Scalper
Resell tickets to an event for a profit.

Tile Installer/Tilesetter
Lay tile for floors and walls.

Timekeeper
Operate the official clock for a sporting event.

Tinsmith
Make various items out of tin.

Tire Changer/Repairer
Repair and rotate tires.

Tire Retreader
Put new treads on used tires.

Tobacconist
Sell tobacco products. A dying occupation.

Toll Collector
Work in a booth collecting fees to allow drivers to use a highway or bridge.

Tool and Die Maker
Make and repair machines in a manufacturing plant.

Top Executive
A leader in a company, like a CEO.

Tour Bus Driver
Drive tourists in a bus to visit various sites of interest.

Tour Guide
Lead a group of visiting people to sites of interest.

Tower Crane Operator
Operate a tall crane to lift and hoist loads into position or to a location.

Toxicologist
Study the effects of radiation and toxic substances on human, animal and plant life.

Trademark Attorney
A specialized lawyer who helps companies protect the symbols that identify their products.

Traffic Controller/Flag Person
Direct non-construction traffic at a construction site.

Training Specialist
Work for a company teaching employees various skills.

Transcriptionist (Medical/Legal)
Record verbal health care records into written form.

Translator
Convert one language to another.

Transmission Mechanic
Repair the transmissions of cars and trucks.

Transport Refrigeration Mechanic
Repair refrigeration units in trucks that move cooled or frozen products.

Transport Trailer Technician
Repair transport trailers used to move goods.

Transportation Security Administration Officer
Ensure the safety of cargo and people on commercial aircraft.

Trapper
Set snares and traps to capture animals for food and pelts.

Travel Agent
Help people with their travel plans.

Travel Writer
Document travel adventures.

Treasurer
Look after the financial records of a company or organization.

Tree Planter
Plant trees in barren areas in an act of reforestation.

Tree Trimmer
Prune trees as part of a landscaping program.

Truck & Transport Vehicle Mechanic
Repair trucks and buses.

Truck Driver (Dump, Semi)
Operate a truck to transport construction material or commercial goods locally or long distance.

Turd Burner Technician
Dispose of human waste in northern communities by burning it in gas-fired burners.

Tutor
Assist students outside the classroom with their studies.

Ufologist
Study unidentified flying objects.

Ultimate Fighter
Compete in mixed martial arts fighting.

Ultrasound Technician/Technologist
Operate ultrasound equipment used in diagnosis.

Umpire
Enforce the rules in a sporting event like baseball.

Undertaker
A funeral director.

Underwater Logger
Salvage submerged logs for timber.

Union Leader
Direct the negotiations between a group of workers and the management of a company or organization.

Upholsterer
Install and repair the fabric and padding on furniture and cushions.

Urban Planner
Direct the development of cities and towns.

Urologist
A doctor who specializes in the urinary tract.

Usher
Assist people to their seats.

Utility Arborist
Clear or prune vegetation that could contact electrical devices or lines.

Valet
Park a customer's car at a restaurant or store.

Valve Installer/Repairer
Install and repair metering devices, gas regulators and various flow valves.

Vending Machine Service and Repair Technician
Repair machines that dispense packaged food or bottled and canned products. Ensure the change return button does not work.

Ventriloquist
An entertainer who manipulates a doll and makes it appear to be talking.

Venture Capitalist
Provide funding for start-up companies in return for some company control and/or profits.

Veterinarian
A doctor who cares for animals.

Video Game Designer
Create video games.

Video Game Player
Enter competitions for money.

Video Game Tester
Play video games for quality assurance.

Video Jockey
An artist who manipulates images on large displays or screens.

Videographer
Record events like weddings with a video camera.

Vintner
A maker of wine.

Violin Maker/Repairer
Make and repair violins.

Violinist
A musician who plays the violin.

Voice Coach
Assist entertainers to improve their singing or speaking voices.

Voiceover Artist
Provide the vocal aspect of a visual commercial, TV show or movie.

Volcanologist
A person who studies volcanoes.

Volleyball Player
Play volleyball professionally.

Volunteer Coordinator
Organize the duties of people who volunteer.

Waiter/Waitress
Serve food and beverages in restaurants and bars.

Wallpaper Hanger
Put designed paper onto walls.

Wardrobe Stylist
A person who picks out the clothing worn by other people in photographs, TV or videos. They may also go to individuals' homes to help people make clothing decisions.

Warehouse Worker
Store and move items in a warehouse.

Waste Picker/Sorter
Work at a recycling plant removing and sorting recyclable material from garbage.

Watch Repairer
Fix clocks and watches.

Watchmaker
Make clocks and watches.

Water Bomber Pilot
Fly a plane that dumps water on forest fires.

Water Well Driller
Drill wells for people so they can have a source of water.

Weapons Designer
Create methods of killing people.

Weather Forecaster
Predict the weather.

Weatherman
Report the current weather and weather predictions on TV or radio.

Weaver
Make rugs or clothing.

Web Designer
Create web sites.

Web Programmer
Write code to be interpreted by web browsers.

Webmaster
A person in charge of a web site.

Wedding Planner
Help people organize their weddings.

Welder/Solderer/Brazier
Join metal together.

Welfare Eligibility Worker
Review welfare applications.

Wellhead Pumper
Operate pumping equipment in oil and gas wells.

Wholesaler
Purchase goods from a manufacturer and sell them to retail stores.

Wig Maker
Make wigs for people who have lost some or all of their hair.

Wildlife Officer
Enforce hunting and fishing laws.

Wind Instrument Repairer
Repair musical instruments.

Window Cleaner
Clean residential or commercial windows.

Window Installer
Put windows in residential and commercial buildings.

Wine Taster
Evaluate wine during winemaking or for suitability in a restaurant or for retail sale.

Winemaker
Someone who makes wine.

Wing Walker
Stand atop the wings of an airplane while in flight.

Woodcarver
An artist who uses sharp metal tools to make designs in wood for furniture, musical instruments or as artwork.

Woodworker
Anyone who makes objects using wood.

Wrangler/Dude Wrangler
A person who handles horses and other animals, or someone who takes people on western horseback riding trips.

Wrestler
An entertainer who wrestles before a crowd.

Writer
Write books, articles or scripts.

X-ray Technician/Technologist
Operate x-ray equipment.

Yardmaster (Rail Yard)
The person in charge at a railroad yard.

Yoga Instructor
Someone who teaches yoga.

Youth Worker
A social worker who works with young people.

Zamboni Operator
Drive a machine to clean the ice surface at an ice rink.

Zookeeper
Care for animals at a zoo.

Zoologist
Study animals.

Conclusion

If you didn't find any jobs to add to your list, go through it again with a more open attitude, and if you have hundreds of career possibilities then you need to pare down that list into something more manageable like ten to twenty.

Take the list of careers you are interested in and use your favourite search engine to find out more information about each career choice. You may find that the job isn't what you thought it would be, so scratch it off and go on to the next one. When you find one that sounds really interesting, circle that one, but continue to work through your list.

When you are researching your career choices, pay more attention to government web sites and be very cautious about any information you find on a site that is promoting a school or an online course. They are often more interested in getting your money than giving you the qualifications you'll need to get a job.

During your research make sure your career area of interest will be growing and not shrinking. It is very disappointing to spend thousands of dollars on an education only to find there are no jobs to be had in your chosen field.

You also need to be realistic about your abilities and level of commitment. If you enjoy sitting in your recreation room playing your guitar and writing songs, that's great. But if you think a record producer is going to bang on your door and sign you to a deal or your uploaded video is going to go viral and you'll be discovered, you will most likely be disappointed.

If you want to be a musician then you need experience playing in front of people and getting feedback. It could be at a local high school battle of the bands night, a local church or busking on the sidewalk downtown. Gaining confidence playing in public is more important than any money you could make at this stage. If you're too afraid or it's too uncomfortable for you to step up into the spotlight then consider your music a hobby and search for something else to do for work.

Check to see if a career involves shift work. If you don't perform well working at different times, then steer away from shift work. You should also consider your physical ability. If the job requires lifting 100-pound blocks of stone at a quarry or 70 to 80 pound bags of shingles if you're a roofer, make sure you can physically handle the workload.

Can any of your career choices be performed as a self employed business? It is a lot more work but self employment can be very rewarding.

Chapter Six

Putting it all Together

Introduction

This is the most important part of your journey because it is here that you will make sense of your wants and desires and ensure that they are congruent.

Congruent means that your choices make sense together. If your ideal house is a $10 million monster house on the ocean and your ideal job is being a librarian, then unless you win the lottery or inherit money, there is no way a librarian could afford a house like that. You will either have to change your ideal house to a small rancher in the suburbs or you will have to change your career to entertainer or sports professional, or any other occupation that could generate enough income to afford such an expensive house.

Goal Making

The rules for making a great goal are to focus on them as if they have already been achieved and to follow a few steps referred to as SMART.

Specific

You have to be very clear on what it is you want to accomplish. If your goal is to "lose some weight," the idea is too vague and your brain will have difficulty coming up with ways to help you.

A better goal would include something like, "I will lose 15 pounds."

Measurable

It's hard to know if you have reached your goal if you are not clear on what the goal is. Instead of "I will run every day," try writing something like, "I will increase my running distance by 10 percent every week until I can run 10 kilometres."

Achievable

If you want to lose 30 pounds and you want to do it in 20 days, then you are probably setting yourself up for failure, because such drastic weight loss in such a short term would be very difficult to achieve and would be unhealthy for you to even attempt.

You didn't gain an extra 30 pounds in less than a month so it will take quite a bit longer than that to safely lose that amount of weight. A realistic and safe weight loss would be one to two pounds a week.

Realistic

If you are 30 years old and 5' 4" and your goal is to play in the NBA or you want to buy a new car with money you'll save from your paper route, then you are not being realistic. Write down what you think the realities of each goal might be. You may find you can adjust the goal statement to make it work better for you. For example, you may realize that being young and tall are requirements for playing in the NBA, but they aren't requirements for coaching, training or scouting.

Time-Based

You should strive to have your goal accomplished by a certain date so your brain will have a time frame to work with. Write something like, "I will learn to swim by July 1st, 2012."

It's also helpful to keep your goal statements positive in their tone and personalize them by using "I" as in "I will enjoy running my first half marathon."

Putting it all together will give you something like:

"I will learn to swim the front crawl the length of the pool by July 1st, 2012 by taking swimming lessons every week."

You now have a definite goal, a realistic time frame and even the basis of a plan to make it all happen.

Some people suggest that you write a goal statement for all of your goals and read them a few times every day. I think reading a huge list of goals every day will not only be time-consuming, but your brain won't be able to wrap itself around so many different things at once.

I suggest that you look over your lists and break them down into short, medium and long term goals. Short term would be within a month or two, medium might be one to two years and long term goals may take five to ten years.

You may also want to think about maintaining balance in your life by considering the following areas of your life when you are deciding on the goals you want to work on:

- Career
- Relationships and family
- Health
- Personal
- Education
- Financial
- Recreation and free time
- Spiritual
- Emotional
- Community and charity

Select one or two short term goals, one or two medium length goals and one or two long term goals from your lists and write a goal statement for just those items. Write each of those on an index card and read it several times a day, especially when you first wake up in the morning and just before going to sleep at night.

A great way to keep all your goals from slipping to the back burner to be forgotten is to make a collage that displays all your goals, and to set up a binder.

Search the internet or browse through magazines and cut out or print a picture that comes as close as possible to representing each of you goals. If you want a 30-foot fishing boat then find one on the internet and print out two copies. Get a large sheet of bristol board and glue one of the pictures onto the sheet, and glue the other one onto a sheet of notebook paper that you can place into a 3-ring binder.

When you have gone through finding pictures for all your goals, you will have an awe-inspiring poster that you can put on your wall and look at every day. You will also have a life-plan binder that you should take out once a month and review. Go to a calm and relaxing place like your local park and sit down and slowly go through your book a page at a time envisioning owning, doing and being everything you dream of.

If you have loving and supportive family and friends and you feel you can share some of your goals with them, that's great. If on the other hand you think it's likely that they will put you down and make fun of your dreams, then by all means keep your goals to yourself.

My mother had the philosophy that "You're wrong and I'm going to tell you all the ways that you're wrong," coupled with an "If you can't find fault with everything, why did you bother getting out of bed this morning?" attitude.

Sharing with her didn't go very well for me. And when someone close to you puts you down you'll want to chuck the whole lot of goals as a waste of time and something you'll never accomplish, and you'll want to give up. People who criticize others for trying to better themselves are often bitter individuals who have never had the courage to follow their own dreams and can only feel good by dragging those around them down.

Don't be surprised if you get the most resistance from your family and friends because, even though they love and care about you, there is also a subconscious envy when someone around them is trying to improve themselves. They may, without realizing it, feel that your efforts to better yourself only serve to emphasize their own failures and un-willingness to change.

You will have to learn to care more about achieving your goals than the opinions of those around you. It's great if you have cheering fans, but don't expect them.

An empowering situation would be if you and a few of your friends each had a copy of this book and you worked through it together, each creating your own personal lists. Then meet once a week and share your successes and fail-ures in a supportive "Goals Club" atmosphere.

If you want to accomplish your goals, you will have to be ready to leave your comfort zone and do some things you are really passionate about or have always wanted to try.

How many great books are left unwritten, works of art not created or inventions left as just an idea in a notebook? How many people come back from an inspiring seminar excited and cranked up just to have the grind of daily life wear them down and beat their dreams out of them?

Most people are just treading water and hoping things will change, but unless you leave your comfort zone and try new things, your life will remain the same. And when you do leave your comfort zone, you will become less fearfull so that eventually your comfort zone will expand to allow you to explore life even further. Something that used to scare you will become second nature and easy for you to do the next time.

Some goals can seem almost impossible to complete because they are so large or complicated. In this case you have to break the goal down into smaller steps for its achievement. If you want to write a book but the idea seems overwhelming, then just write one page a day and in a year's time you'll have written a book.

You may think a goal like starting your own business will requires you to do a million things. Get out a pad of paper and a pen and write down all the things you can think of that need to be done. You may find the list has 62 things on it. That's great! You just went from a million to 62 and now the task doesn't seem as daunting.

To accomplish your goals you will also have to work on them every day. A new car isn't going to show up in your driveway as a result of you having positive, happy thoughts.

While working on your goals you will also need to develop persistence. You will experience setbacks so be prepared for them. Just step back, take a break, regroup and try again. So many people give up when they are very close to success because of a lack of persistence. If life knocks you down five times then get up six.

To keep yourself motivated, don't wait until you have reached your goal, but reward yourself after every milestone, or when a significant step has been completed. Buy a small charm, go out to a movie or pick up an item of clothing.

When you do accomplish one of your goals then celebrate it! You may order some takeout or head off for a three-day weekend. Learn to pat yourself on the back for a job well done. Record your success on the "Success" page of your binder or notebook, and if a tough time comes and you are feeling discouraged, read over this page and feel good about all the things you have accomplished.

Your list of goals will also change over time. Something you may have wanted may not seem important anymore and other items will come up that you will want to add. No worries, that's part of life.

Any plan is better than no plan, and by now you should have several SMART goal statements that put your own personal life plan in a clear light. Feel free to change anything that is not working for you. Take any setback as feedback and use it as an opportunity to grow.

I wish you all the success you deserve, and remember to enjoy the journey.

———•+•———

To Order Books

Individual orders for paperback and ebooks and bulk orders for PTAs, graduation classes, sales promotional use and corrections institutions can be found at:

www.GoalsForChange.com/ordering